Alexander Bain

Mind and body

The theories of their relation

Alexander Bain

Mind and body
The theories of their relation

ISBN/EAN: 9783741163074

Manufactured in Europe, USA, Canada, Australia, Japa

Cover: Foto ©berggeist007 / pixelio.de

Manufactured and distributed by brebook publishing software
(www.brebook.com)

Alexander Bain

Mind and body

MIND AND BODY.

THE THEORIES

OF THEIR

RELATION.

BY

ALEXANDER BAIN, L.L.D.,

PROFESSOR OF LOGIC IN THE UNIVERSITY OF ABERDEEN.

LONDON :

HENRY S. KING & Co.,

65, CORNHILL, AND 12, PATERNOSTER ROW.

1873.

CONTENTS.

—◆—

MIND AND BODY.

CHAPTER I.

QUESTION STATED.

MANY persons, mocking, ask—What has Mind to do with brain substance, white and grey? Can any facts or laws regarding the spirit of man be gained through a scrutiny of nerve fibres and nerve cells?

The question, whatever may be insinuated in putting it, is highly relevant, and raises great issues.

. The conceivable answers are various :—

First. Granting mind and body to be in our present life inseparable, yet the two might be supposed to have their modes of existence altogether distinct, the one being wholly unaffected by the other. Consequently, each would have to be studied in its own way, and for its own sake alone. On this supposition, the study of brain matter might be interesting as Physiology and for applications

B

to Medicine and Surgery, but would be quite beyond the province of the mental philosopher.

Although no intrinsic improbability attaches to this supposition, it is scarcely in accordance with what we find in the usual course of things. There is no example of two agents so closely united as mind and body, without some mutual interference or adaptation. Still, the union of our incorporeal and corporeal parts is a case quite peculiar, not to say unique; and we are not entitled to pronounce beforehand as to the behaviour of two such agents in respect of each other.

Secondly. There might be certain mental functions of a *lower* kind, partially dependent upon the material organization, while the highest functions might be of a purely spiritual nature, in no way governed by physical conditions. For receiving impressions, in the first instance, we need the External Senses; we are dependent on the constitution and working of the Eye, the Ear, the organ of Touch, and so on; yet the deeper processes named Memory, Reason, Imagination—may be pure spirit, beyond and apart from all material processes. In such a case, the enquirer into mind would do well to study the mechanism of the Senses; but, for the purpose he has in view, it would be needless to go farther.

Thirdly. There may be an intimate relation and dependence of mind and body all through, every mental act having a concurrent bodily change; yet the two

modes of operation may be so different as to throw
no light on each other. No great laws may be traceable
on either side, or the laws may be couched in such
heterogeneous terms that we can make no comparison
of the two. A pleasure and a nervous current are found
to arise simultaneously; but the concurrence (we may
suppose) signifies nothing, suggests nothing. There is
something to be gained by connecting pleasure with
a repast, a concert, or a holiday; but the mention of
nerve currents gives no information of a practical kind,
and does not add to our knowledge of the laws of pleasure.

Fourthly. While allowing it to be possible that a
thorough understanding of the brain would contribute
to a knowledge of the mind, one might deny that anything yet known, or in immediate prospect of being
known, is of value in that way. Thus the obtrusion of
physiology at the present stage would be superfluous
and impotent.

Fifthly. The position may be taken that a knowledge
of the bodily workings has already improved our knowledge of the mental workings, and, as we continue our
researches, will do so more and more.

Which of these suppositions is the truth could be seen
only after examining the actual state of the case. On a
theme so peculiar and so difficult, the only surmise
admissible beforehand would be, that the two distinct
natures could not subsist in their present intimate
alliance, and yet be wholly indifferent to one another;

that they would be found to have some kind of mutual co-operation; that the ongoings of the one would be often a clue to the ongoings of the other.

The form of the interrogation that the foregoing remarks are designed to answer, may be objected to as purely rhetorical and in some measure unfair. If the matter of the brain were the only substance that mental functions could be attributed to, all the knowledge that we possess of that organ might not avail us much in laying down laws of connexion between mind and body. But such is not the fact. The entire bodily system, though in varying degrees, is in intimate alliance with mental functions. To confine our study to the nervous substance would be to misrepresent the connexion; and the knowledge of that substance, however complete, would not suffice for the solution of the problem. Looking at a child's cut finger, we can divine its feelings; if we see a smiling countenance, we know something of the mental tone of the individual.

It might seem that we must yet be a long way from understanding an organ so minute and so complicated as the Brain. If we were to confine ourselves to the one mode of post-mortem dissection, we should probably attain but a small measure of success. But another road is open. We can begin at the outworks, at the organs of sense and motion, with which the nervous system communicates; we can study their operations during life, as well as examine their intimate structure; we can experimentally vary all the circumstances of their operation ; we can find how they act upon the brain, and how the brain re-acts upon them. Using all this knowledge as a key, we may possibly unlock the secrets of the anatomical structure ; we may compel the cells and fibres to disclose their meaning and purpose.

CHAPTER II.

CONNEXION OF MIND AND BODY.

THE facts showing that the connexion of Mind and Body is not occasional or partial, but thorough-going and complete, are such as the following .

In the first place, it has been noted in all ages and countries, that the Feelings possess a natural language or Expression. So constant are the appearances characterizing the different classes of emotions, that we regard them as a part of the emotions themselves.

The smile of joy, the puckered features in pain, the stare of astonishment, the quivering of fear, the tones and glance of tenderness, the frown of anger,—are united in seemingly inseparable association with the states of feeling that they indicate. If a feeling arises without its appropriate sign or accompaniment, we account for the failure either by voluntary suppression, or by the faintness of the excitement, there being a certain degree or intensity requisite to affect the bodily organs.*

* The following remarks of Mr. Darwin are in point :—Most of our emotions [he should have said all] are so closely connected with their expression, that they hardly exist if the body remains passive. A man, for instance, may know that his life is in the extremest peril, and may strongly desire to save it ; yet, as Louis XVI. said, when surrounded by

On this uniformity of connexion between feelings and their bodily expression depends our knowledge of each other's mind and character. When anyone is pleased, or pained, or loving, or angry, unless there is purposed concealment, we are aware of the fact, and can even estimate in any given case the degree of the feeling.

From a variety of causes, we are deeply interested in the outward display of emotion. The face of inanimate nature does not arrest our attention so strongly as the deportment of our fellow beings; in truth, the highest attraction of natural objects is imparted to them by a fictitious process of investing them with human feelings. The sun and the moon, the winds and the rivers, are less engaging when viewed as mere physical agencies, than when they are supposed to operate by human motives and purposes, loves and hates.

The interest of the human presence, in all its various workings, regarded as symptomatic of mental processes, is laid hold of and heightened in the Fine Art of cultivated nations. To the painter, the sculptor, and the poet, every feeling has its appropriate manifestation. Not merely are the grosser forms of feeling thus linked

a fierce mob, "Am I afraid? feel my pulse." So a man may intensely hate another; but until his bodily frame is affected, he cannot be said to be enraged. ('Expression,' p. 239.)

To the like effect Dr. Maudsley observes:—"The special muscular action is not merely the exponent of the passion, but truly an essential part of it. If we try, while the features are fixed in the expression of one passion, to call up in the mind a different one, we shall find it impossible to do so." ('Body and Mind,' p. 30.)

with material adjuncts ; in the artist's view, the loftiest,
the noblest, the holiest of the human emotions, have their
marked and inseparable attitude and deportment.   In the
artistic conceptions of the Middle Ages, more especially,
the most divine attributes of the immaterial soul had their
counterpart in the material body: the martyr, the saint,
the blessed Virgin, the Saviour Himself, manifested their
glorious nature by the sympathetic movements of the
mortal framework.   So far as concerns the entire compass
of our feelings or emotions, it is the universal testimony
of mankind that these have no independent spiritual sub-
sistence, but are in every case embodied in our fleshly form.

This very strong and patent fact has been usually kept
out of view in the multifarious discussions respecting the
Immaterial Soul. Apparent as it is to the vulgar, and
intently studied as it has been by the sculptor, the
painter, and the poet, it has been disregarded both by
metaphysicians and by theologians when engaged in
settling the boundaries of mind and body.

A second class of proofs of the intimate connexion
between Mind and Body is furnished by the effects of
bodily changes on mental states, and of mental changes on
bodily states.

The embarrassment in dealing with this group of facts
is their number. I shall commence with a few of the
ordinary and recognised instances, and then refer to the
comprehensive generalities arrived at by physiologists.

As to the influence of bodily changes on Mental states, we have such facts as the dependence of our feelings and moods upon hunger, repletion, the state of the stomach, fatigue and rest, pure and impure air, cold and warmth, stimulants and drugs, bodily injuries, disease, sleep, advancing years. These influences extend not merely to the grosser modes of feeling, and to such familiar exhibitions as after-dinner oratory, but also to the highest emotions of the mind—love, anger, æsthetic feeling, and moral sensibility. "Health keeps an Atheist in the dark." Bodily affliction is often the cause of a total change in the moral nature.

The bodily routine of our daily life is the counterpart of the mental routine. A healthy man wakens in the morning with a flush of spirits and energy ; his first meal confirms and re-inforces the state. The mental powers and susceptibilities are then at their maximum ; as the nutrition is used up in the system, they gradually fade, but may be renewed once and again by refreshment and brief remission of toil. Towards the end of the day lassitude sets in, and fades into the deep unconsciousness of healthy sleep.

Since the Intellectual faculties appear to be most removed from the effect of physical agencies, I will quote a few facts, showing that in reality they have no exemption from the general rule. The memory rises and falls with the bodily condition ; being vigorous in our fresh moments, and feeble when we are fatigued or exhausted. It is related by Sir Henry Holland that on one occasion he descended, on the same day, two deep mines in the Hartz mountains, remaining some hours in each. In the second mine he was so exhausted with inanition and fatigue, that his memory utterly failed him ; he could not recollect a single word of German. The power came back after taking food and wine. Old age notoriously impairs the memory in ninety-nine men out of a hundred.

In the delirium of fever the sense of hearing sometimes becomes extraordinarily acute. Among the premonitory symptoms of brain disease has been noticed an unusual delicacy of the sense of sight ; the physician suspects that there is already congestion of blood, to be followed perhaps by effusion.

Any person fancying that trains of thinking have little dependence on the bodily organs should also reflect on such facts as these. When walking, or engaged in any bodily occupation, if an interesting idea occurs to the mind, or is imparted to us by another person, we suddenly stop, and remain at rest, until the excitement has subsided. Again, our cogitations usually induce some bodily attitudes (laid hold of by artists as the outward expression of Thought) as well as movements ; and if anything occurs to disturb these, the current of thinking is suspended or diverted. Why should sleep suspend all thought, except the incoherency of dreaming (absent in perfect sleep), if a certain condition of the bodily powers were not indispensable to the intellectual functions ?

Much stress has been laid upon certain apparent exceptions to these sweeping rules. Under bodily weakness, abstinence, fatigue, disease, and old age, individuals occasionally manifest high mental energy and elation, and great intellectual power. The lives of martyrs and heroes are replete with such exceptional vigour. If the inference be that the mind, notwithstanding a large amount of dependence on the body, is still, to a certain degree, self-supporting and independent, we must ask why the fact should be exhibited only in a few rare cases? The supposition resembles in partiality and capriciousness the Platonic Immortality, conferred only on philosophers. Still, any complete view of the relations of Mind and Body should take account of these striking exceptions; and we shall revert to them at a later stage.

The influence of mental changes upon the Body is supported by an equal force of testimony. Sudden outbursts of emotion derange the bodily functions. Fear paralyzes the digestion. Great mental depression enfeebles all the organs. Protracted and severe mental labour brings on disease of the bodily organs. On the other hand, happy outward circumstances are favourable to health and longevity.

In the personifications so common in our early poetry the various passions are described by the marks that their long dominance leaves on the bodily figure. In Sackville's "Induction," Dread is described as follows :—

Next saw we Dread all trembling, how he shook,
  With foot uncertain proffer'd here and there :
Denumb'd of speech, and, with a ghastly look,
  Search'd every place, all pale and dead for fear.

And Misery :—

His face was lean, and some deal pined away,
And eke his hands consumed to the bone.

In considering minutely the evidences of the connexion
of mind and body, we gradually perceive that the organ
most intimately associated with mind is the BRAIN. Other
organs have been assigned, at various times, as the special
seats of mental activity, but these are now abandoned.
Yet, although the Brain is by pre-eminence the mental
organ, other organs co-operate; more especially, the Senses,
the Muscles, and the great Viscera.

The peculiar structure of the Brain will be afterwards
adverted to. For the present, I remark that it is a very
large and complicated organ; it receives a copious supply
of blood, computed as one-fifth of the entire circulation, a circumstance betokening great activity of some
kind or other. Now the facts that connect the mind with
the brain are numerous and irresistible. Let us rehearse .
a few of them, under the two aspects already stated; brain
changes affecting the mind, mental changes affecting the
brain.

Under the first topic, the commonest observation is the
effect of a blow on the head, which suspends for the
time consciousness and thought; at a certain pitch of
severity it produces a permanent injury of the faculties,

impairing the memory, or occasioning some form of mental derangement. It may also *remedy* derangement; there are cases on record, where a blow on the head has cured Idiocy.

All those abuses and casualties that impair the mental faculties act upon the nervous substance. Thus, stimulating drugs operate upon the nerves. Many instances of imbecility of mind are distinctly traced to causes affecting the nutrition of the brain.

The more careful and studied observations of physiologists have shewn beyond question that the brain as a whole is indispensable to thought, to feeling, and to volition; while they have further discriminated the functions of its different parts.

Next, as regards mental changes leading to brain changes, or being associated with them, we can quote very extensive observations. Thus, after great mental exertion or excitement, there is an increase of the products of nervous waste. The alkaline phosphates removed from the blood by the kidneys are derived from the brain and nerves; and these are increased after severe exercise of the mind.

Again, violent emotions are among the causes of paralysis, which is a disease of the nerves or nerve centres.

Most decisive of all, under this head, is the wide experience of the insane. Among the chief causes of

insanity must be reckoned excessive drafts on the mind —
as, for example, long and severe mental exertion, and
sudden mental shocks, usually of disaster and misfortune,
but occasionally even of joy.

The association of brain-derangement with mind-de-
rangement is all but a perfectly established induction. In
the great mass of insane patients the alteration of the brain
is visible and pronounced. I may quote as evidence on
this head a pamphlet by Drs. J. B. Tuke and Rutherford,
"On the Morbid Appearances met with in the Brains of
Thirty Insane Persons." 'The brains examined were those
of patients whose deaths occurred consecutively, and were
in no way picked on account of any peculiarity.' The
forms of disease exemplified were general paralysis, dementia with paralysis, chronic dementia, epileptic insanity. *In every case there was noticed a marked departure in one form or another from the healthy structure of
the brain.* The authors enumerate nine species of morbid
changes, discovered by microscopical examination. The
occurrence of a case that presented no visible derangement would not be a conclusive exception, inasmuch as
there may be alterations of substance that are not
visible. It is believed, however, that in all cases of
pronounced mental aberration, disease of the brain is
present in a marked form.

A very instructive class of facts may be adduced, connecting mental action with the quantity and quality of

the *blood* supplied to the brain. No organ is active without blood. The demand made by the brain corresponds with the extent and energy of its functions. Deficiency in the circulation is accompanied with feeble manifestations of mind. In sleep, there is a diminution of the supply of arterial blood to the brain. General depletion lowers all the functions generally, mind included. On the other hand, when the cerebral circulation is quickened, the feelings are roused, the thoughts are more rapid, the volitions more vehement; great mental excitement is always accompanied with an unusual flow of blood, often outwardly shown by the throbbing of the vessels. In delirium, the circulation attains an extraordinary pitch.

The blood must possess a certain *quality*, involving the presence of certain ingredients and the absence of others. Wholesome nourishment supplies the first condition of nervous and mental activity; inanition or starvation, feebleness of digestion, militate against the exercise of the mental functions. Moreover, the blood may be abundant and rich in nutritive matters, yet the organ of the mind may be unduly depressed by the excessive drafts of the other interests of the system, as, for example, the muscles; under great muscular strain, there is very little capability of mental effort. Again, there are certain substances, known as stimulants, that are considered to supply the blood with an element specially provocative of nervous change; as alcohol, tobacco, tea, opium, &c.

The substances that must be absent include the so-called

poisons, and the impurities of the body itself, which several large viscera are occupied in removing.   The chief of these impurities are carbonic acid and urea; either of them left to accumulate in the blood leads to mental depression, unconsciousness, and finally death.   Hence the mental tone depends no less upon the vigorous condition of the purifying organs—lungs, liver, intestines, kidneys, skin —than upon the presence of nutritive material obtained from the food.

CHAPTER III.

THE CONNEXION VIEWED AS CORRESPONDENCE, OR CONCOMITANT VARIATION.

THE dependence of one thing upon another, is ordinarily shown by two classes of facts—the first, the presence of the cause followed by the presence of the effect; the second, the absence of the cause followed by the absence of the effect: as when we prove that lighting a fire is the cause of smoke, or oxygen the cause of putrefaction and decay. Of the two methods, the second—the absence of the cause followed by the absence of the effect—is the most decisive; the preservation of meat by excluding air is the best proof that air, or some ingredient of it, is the cause of putrefaction. More especially convincing is the abrupt removal of a supposed cause, leading at once to the suspension of an effect.

There are cases, however, where we cannot make the experiment of removing an agent. We cannot get away from the earth where we live. We cannot remove the moon from its sphere, so as to see what actions on the earth depend upon it; we cannot by an abrupt suspension of lunar gravitation prove that the tides are very largely dependent on lunar influence.

C

For such cases, recourse is had to a third expedient,
which happily solves the difficulty, and furnishes the proof
required.   If the agency in question, although irremov-
able, passes through gradations whose amount can be
measured, we are able to observe whether the effect has
corresponding changes of degree; and if a strict concomitance is observable between the intensity of the cause and
the intensity of the effect, we have a presumption that may
rise to positive proof of the connexion. It is thus shown that
the tides depend on the moon and the sun conjointly ; that
the gaseous and liquid states of matter are due to heat.

In such a question as the connexion of mind and body,
the potent method of removing the cause is not applicable.   We cannot dissect the compound, man, into body
apart and mind apart; we cannot remove mind so as to
see if the body will vanish. We may remove the body, and
in so doing we find that mind has disappeared ; but the
experiment is not conclusive ; for, in removing the body
we remove our indicator of the mind, namely, the bodily
manifestations—as if in testing for magnetism we should
set aside the needle and other tokens of its presence.

Neither can the method of absence be employed upon
the chief organ of mind—the brain.   The removal of the
brain is undoubtedly the extinction of the manifestations
of mind, but it is also, except in very low organisms,
the extinction of the bodily life.   Important results are
gained by partial removal of the brain, and we can reason

from these to what would happen by removing the whole. This is the nearest approach we can make to the best form of experimental proof.

The method of Concomitance or Correspondence is, however, applicable to the full extent. We can compare the gradations of the brain and nervous system through the animal series, and observe whether there are like gradations in the powers of the mind.

A considerable time has elapsed since attention was called by phrenologists to the connexion between size of brain and mental development in human beings. The large heads of men distinguished for high intellectual endowments, or for great energy of character in other ways, have been contrasted with the small heads of idiots. The rule is not strictly maintained in every instance; occasionally a stupid man has a larger brain than a clever man. But these are only individual exceptions to a prevailing arrangement. When extensive statistics are taken, the conclusion is established that great mental superiority is accompanied with a more than average size of brain.

The following is a table of the brain weights of several distinguished men :—

Cuvier	.	.	.	64·5 oz.
Dr. Abercrombie	.	.	.	63 „
Daniel Webster		.	.	53·5 „
Lord Campbell	.	.	.	53·5 „
De Morgan	.	.	.	52·75 „
Gauss	.	,	.	52·6 „

The average male brain (in Europeans) is 49½ oz., the female 44 oz.   (Quain's Anatomy, 7th edition, p. 571).

Among idiots have been found brains weighing 27 oz., 25¾ oz., 22½ oz., 19¾ oz., 18¼ oz., 15 oz., 13 oz., 8½ oz.

According to Dr. Thurnam (*Journal of Mental Science* for 1866), the brains of insane persons are 2½ per cent. below the average of the sane.

The concomitance of size of nervous system with mental power, throughout the animal series, is sufficiently admitted for the purpose of our general argument.   The agreement is not strict, because the nervous system serves other functions besides those that are purely mental.   The mere propulsion of the muscles demands a large supply of nerve force, and animals whose muscles are large and active have correspondingly large brains.   Thus it is that the maximum size of the brain is reached, not in human beings, but in the elephant tribe, and after them the whales, whose ponderous bodies demand an enormous muscular expenditure.   The elephant's brain weighs from 8 to 10 pounds.   The whale's brain is said to weigh from 5 to 8 pounds.   The brain of one 75 feet long was found to weigh 7 pounds; Dr. Struthers found the brain of a young whale, 14½ feet long, 3 lbs. 12 oz., of a tusk whale or sea-unicorn 17 feet long, 3 lbs. 14¾ oz.

In addition to propulsion of the muscles, a considerable amount of nerve force must be expended in supporting or aiding the processes of organic life—digestion, respiration, circulation, and other operations. The strongest proof on this point is the very great falling off in these various functions when the nerve force is monopolized for intense mental or muscular exertion.

It is found that tall men, as a rule, have larger brains than small men.

Comparing the increasing size of the brain with the increase in mental power, we are struck with the smallness of the one increase as compared with the other. An ordinary male human brain is 48 oz.; the brains of extraordinary men seldom reach Cuvier's figure, 64 oz. Now the intellectual force of the ordinary man is surpassed by Cuvier in a far higher ratio than this. Taking the mere memory, which is the basis of intellect, an ordinary man could not retain one-third or one-fourth, perhaps not one-tenth, of the facts stored up in the mind of a Cuvier. The comparison of animals with human beings would sustain a similar inference. There would be no exaggeration in saying that while size of brain increases in arithmetical proportion, intellectual range increases in geometrical proportion.

A still more important and suggestive correspondence is discernible in the manner of working of the nervous system. Notwithstanding the radical distinction of nature between bodily action and mental action, we are surprised to see how closely certain circumstances of the one are conjoined with similar circumstances of the other. To understand this argument, a brief consideration must be given to the plan or mechanism of the nervous system.

Undoubtedly the best way of approaching the nervous structure is to commence from outside appearances. Every one is aware of the existence of sense organs and of moving organs; and more than that, each of us could recount a great many minute particulars respecting both classes. Now a study of these familiar facts suggests some of the deepest arrangements of the nervous structure.

The Sense Organs, usually reckoned five in number, are all more or less open to view. The organ of the sense of touch is the entire covering or integument of the body, the skin. The others are confined to special localities. By a sense organ is meant a portion of the body exposed to certain agents, and, when stimulated, giving birth to feelings of the mind. Each sense is suited to a particular class of influences: Touch to solid pressures; Hearing to aerial pressures; Taste to liquid or dissolved matters having certain properties of a chemical nature; Smell to gaseous effluvia of a like nature; Sight to the rays of the sun or other luminous bodies.

The Moving Organs are all parts of the body—head, face, eyes, mouth, throat, neck, back, arms, legs, &c., &c. Every one of these goes through a great variety of changes of posture, alternations, combinations, and with greater or less rapidity and continuance. The motions are nearly all visible to the eye. The moving agents are concealed from outward view, but can be easily got at by dissection. The red flesh of meat, called muscular tissue, is a stringy substance made up into separate masses called muscles, of the most various shapes and sizes, but all agreeing in one property, called contractility or forcible shrinking. A muscle has its two extremities attached to bones or other parts, and in contracting it draws the two attachments nearer one another, and thereby effects the movements that we see. A broad spreading muscle placed over the temple and attached to the skull at one end, and at the other end to the lower jaw, when under contraction, closes the jaw in biting; the closure being accomplished with a certain energy, according to the size of the muscle and other circumstances. The large muscles of the fore part of the thigh are so placed as to straighten the leg when bent at the knee. The numerous movements of the human hand need a corresponding number of muscles. There are between four and five hundred muscles in the human body.

We must next consider the mutual relationship of these two sets of organs, Sense Organs and Moving Organs. Something needs to act upon a sense organ in order that we may get a sensation ; and something needs to act upon a moving organ, or a muscle, in order to a movement. Both the one and the other are of themselves inactive or quiescent. The stimulus of the sense organs is generally apparent ; a solid body touching the skin, a morsel in the

mouth, a perfume to the nostrils, and so on. The stimulants of the moving organs are not so apparent: their
origin is internal.

We are familiar with a large class of instances, where
a sense stimulus seems also to be a motor stimulus. A
light anywhere appearing suddenly makes us turn to look
at it. A morsel on the tongue awakens all the movements
of mastication. Let us examine the facts more closely.
My hand is lying quiescent on the table; something
touches it lightly, a fly, or a feather; there is a rush of
activity to certain muscles, and the hand is moved away.
Well, supposing the two things to be remote cause and
effect: the light contact—cause, the motion—effect: what
may we suppose as to the *intermediate* links? Unless
the process be something quite unique, there must be a
channel of communication between the skin of the hand
and the group of muscles in the shoulder, upper arm,
and forearm, that unite to withdraw the hand. Assuming
the concurrence of ten muscles, there must be a ramifying
thread of communication from any point in the skin of
the hand to all these ten muscles. If a similar effect were
to occur in the foot, the part moved would be the leg,
showing lines of communication between the skin of the
foot or leg and the muscles of the hip, thigh, and leg, of
which a certain group concur in the single effect of with-
drawing the foot.

Suppose now, instead of a light contact, the hand is
sharply pinched in the very same place. The previous

case shows the evidence of lines of communication between the skin of the hand and a group of muscles of the shoulder and arm, and we are prepared for a similar manifestation, perhaps more violent. We are not disappointed as to the violence ; the same group of muscles appear to be roused, and to act more strongly ; the withdrawal of the hand is greatly quickened. We find, however, that this is not all. With the mere arm movements are coupled a great many more—in the other arm, the legs, the body, and the face, besides the more concealed movements shown in the voice, which emits a cry, shout, or other exclamation. We see that any part of the skin of the hand is in connexion with perhaps two hundred muscles ; the notable circumstance being that a weak touch does not arouse the wider circle of movements. At all events, here is a fact showing the exceedingly numerous and complicated communications between a given portion of the skin and the moving organs. The complication grows upon us as we pursue our reflections upon ordinary facts. We remark that a similar pinch upon any part of the skin—hands, arms, legs, back—will induce a similar wave of effects ; so that every portion of the integument of the body has its lines of communication with a very large number of muscles. Nay, farther, if we try similar experiments upon the other senses, we shall find similar effects ; with a slight application, a limited class of movements ; with a severe application, a wide display identical in general character with those due to a pinch of the skin. A very bitter taste, a malodour, a screeching discord, an intense flame, will each awaken movements of limbs, body, face, and voice. Every one of the senses is in the same extensive communication with the organs of motion.

The effects of a sense stimulation are not ended in a mere jump or attitude performed by a particular group of muscles; very often there is a long succession of movements and attitudes. This raises the complication still farther. The impetus of the sensation is sufficient to stimulate first one movement, then another, and another; showing a new class of lines of communication—those between the moving organs themselves. The bending of an arm is followed by its straightening; the closing of the jaws is succeeded by a lateral grinding motion. Now continuous movements cannot be maintained without a definite communication between each movement and its successor; walking and flying are rendered possible by an arrangement for connecting each movement with the one that regularly follows it.

It is needless, at this stage, to probe deeper that system of complicated intercommunication between sense organs and moving organs, and between one set of moving organs and another, involving hundreds or thousands of connexions. These are as yet mere matter of inference; seeing that an effect is regularly followed by another at a distance, we presume the existence of some means of conveying an agency or force between the two localities. Not till we examine the interior of the body do we know what is the medium employed. On such examination we discover a set of silvery threads, or cords of various sizes, ramifying from centres to all parts of the body, including both sense-surfaces and muscles. These are the *nerves*. The centres whence they ramify are constituted by one large continuous lump, principally of the same silvery material, occupying the skull or cranium as a rounded mass, and continuing into the back bone as a long flattened rod, about half an inch across. The mass in the skull is the brain; the rod in the back bone is the spinal cord. The vastly numerous inter-communications, above shadowed forth, are effected through the nerves and these central masses.

The centres are, in by far the largest part, made up of the same material as the nerve threads; they contain, however, an additional material. To the eye this second material has a different tint, an ashy grey appearance, as is seen by cutting into any portion of the brain or spinal cord of a man or an animal. This visible difference enables us to trace the distribution, and discover the proportions of the two kinds of material. In the brain of man and of the higher animals, we see a curious arrangement of the surface into ridges and furrows, called convolutions, running in various directions; and the convoluted surface consists of a thin uniform cake of the grey substance, while the interior mass is principally made up of the white nervous matter.

The peculiarities of these two sorts of material have

been exhaustively studied, and the significance of both is more or less perfectly ascertained or surmised.

Under the microscope, the White matter, constituting the nerve-threads wholly and the centres in great part, is seen to consist of *fibres* or very minute threads, every visible nerve being a bundle of these. The Grey matter is a mixture of these fibres with a distinct class of bodies, called *cells, vesicles,* or *corpuscles*—small solid bodies, round, pear-shaped, or irregular, with prolongations to connect them with the nerves. These two elements—fibres and cells—together with enclosing membranes, blood-vessels, and cellular tissue, make up the nervous system, both centres and ramifications.

The first significant feature of the two nervous elements is the SIZE. Both are exceedingly minute. The large mass of nerve-substance is an aggregation of a very great number of very small fibres and corpuscles. The fibres range in thickness from $\frac{1}{13000}$ to $\frac{1}{74000}$ of an inch, the medium or average being $\frac{1}{8000}$ of an inch. There are two varieties of fibres; the chief, named " white," or "tubular" fibres, appear to consist each (1) of an outer structureless membrane ; (2) of an interior surrounding layer of fatty matter ; (3) of a central core or cylinder, which is not fatty, but albuminous (nitrogenous, or protein) in composition. To this central axis is attached the proper function of the fibres ; and at the two extremities of the nerves the axis appears alone, divested of its two envelopes : it does not exceed $\frac{1}{100,000}$ of an inch in thickness.

The *cells* or *corpuscles* are of various shapes,—round, oval, pear-shaped, tailed, and star-like or radiated. They consist of pulpy matter, with an eccentric roundish body or nucleus, enclosing one or more smaller nuclei, surrounded by coloured granules. They range from $\frac{1}{300}$ to $\frac{1}{3000}$ of an inch in diameter. Although from the smallness in the amount of the grey matter as compared with the white, and from the greater diameter of the corpuscles, the number of these, in a cross section, is less than the number of fibres, yet as they lie in three dimensions, while the nerves lie only in two, their numerical aggregate is much beyond the aggregate of branching nerve-fibres, although not so great as the total number of fibrous connexions.

The diagram Fig. I, on the next page, represents the cell in its various leading forms.

We may now judge of the immense *multiplication* of nervous elements in the brain and nerves. Estimates have been made of the number of fibres in individual nerves. The third cerebral nerve (the common motor of the eye) is supposed to have as many as fifteen thousand fibres. In the sensory nerves the fibres are smaller; and in the large nerve of sight, the optic nerve, the number must be very great, probably not less than one hundred thousand, and perhaps much more. The number of fibres making up the white substance of the brain must be counted by hundreds of millions.

In this enormous multiplication of independent nerve-elements we seem to have the suitable provision for the vast number of communications needed in the ordinary actions of human beings, as above exemplified.

There are some significant facts regarding the ARRANGE-MENT of the nerve-elements.   It is to be noted, first, that the nerve-fibres proceed from the nerve-centres to the extremities of the body without a break, and without

FIG. 1.*

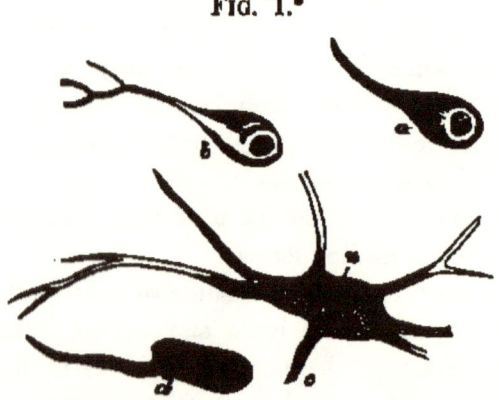

uniting or fusing with one another; so that each unfailingly delivers its separate message.   Without this, the greatness of their number would not give variety of communication.   The chief use of the two coatings

* Nucleated nerve-cells magnified 170 diameters ; a and b from the cerebellum ; c and d from the medulla oblongata ; n the nucleus of a cell.

In Chap. V. a diagram is given (fig. 3) showing the continuation of the fibres into the corpuscles or cells.

or envelopes appears to be to secure the isolation of the
central axis.

Remark, next, that the plan of communicating from
one part of the body to another,—as from the skin of
the hand to the muscles of the arm,—is not by a direct
route from the one spot to the other, but by a nervous
centre. Every nerve-fibre rising from the surface of the
body, or from the eye or the ear, goes first of all to the
spinal cord or to some part of the brain ; and any influence
exerted on the movements by stimulating these fibres
passes out from some nervous centre. As in the circulation
of letters by post, there is no direct communication
between one street and another, but every letter passes
first to the central office, so the transmission of influence
from one member of the body to another is exclusively
through a centre, or (with a few exceptions) through some
part of the nervous substance contained in the head and
backbone. Every communication is centralized ; and, in
consequence, there is not only great economy of the
conducting machinery, but also an avoidance of conflicting
messages.

When we speak of the nerves all ending in the nervous
centres, we mean the *grey* substance, or the aggregate
of fibres and corpuscles. Every nerve ends in a corpuscle ;
and from the same corpuscle arises some other fibre or fibres
either proceeding back to the body direct, or proceeding
to other corpuscles, whence new fibres arise, with the
same alternative. Of the fibres of the brain and spinal cord

the greater number connect corpuscle with corpuscle; a small number go outwards to the muscles, forming the pathway of communication with the moving members.

The Corpuscles are thus the medium of connexion of in-going with out-going nerves, and hence of communication between the outlying parts of the body. In them is organized that system of complicated correspondence, whereby an influence in one part can arouse a wave of effects in many other parts. They are the crossings or grand junctions, where each part can multiply its connexions with the remaining parts. There is not a muscle of the body that could not be reached directly or indirectly by a pressure on the tip of the fore-finger; and this ramified connexion is effected through the nerve-cells or corpuscles; just as, by means of the distribution of post-offices and lines of road, a letter from any village in Europe can be speedily sent to any other village.

A third point to be noted regarding the nerve elements —fibre and corpuscle—is their MATERIAL, composition, or quality. The active part (the core or central axis) of the fibres is composed of particles of an albuminous substance. The corpuscles are also made up of the same material, combined with fatty substances in granules. The substance of both is highly unstable, or easily acted on by external influences of every kind; but of the two elements the corpuscles are considered the most susceptible to change. We can but dimly conceive the precise mode of change that goes on in the one or in the other; it is a change that, when once begun, propagates itself along the whole line of open communications; and it is a change that finds a certain limit only by altering the structure of the nerve. The restoration from the altered structure is due to the blood, which circulates largely among nerve-fibres, but still more largely in the grey matter which contains the corpuscles; it has been computed (Herbert Spencer) that five times as much blood circulates in the grey or corpuscular substance as in the white or fibrous substance. In these imperfectly understood changes of the nerve-tissue, we have the embodiment of what is called the nerve-force. This is an agent with various powers—mechanical agency, heat agency, chemical agency; all which are due to the molecular alteration of the nerve-substance, the complement of the change being a supply of blood in proportion to the force set free.

To return now to the tracing of correspondence and concomitance between mental acts and bodily changes. One grand correspondence is already implied, which will be afterwards more fully discussed—the variety and multitude of our mental acts on the one hand, and the multitude of nervous elements on the other. If our nervous system consisted at most of one thousand ultimate fibres, and one thousand corpuscles, nobody could show how these could be manipulated so as to execute all the variety of the outward manifestations of feelings and thoughts. But great as is the number and variety of mental states, the nervous system, in its prodigious extent and multiplication, seems to show a correspondence by no means inadequate.

The correspondence of number of elements with complicacy of function is seen to advantage in the senses. The nerve of sight is the largest of the nerves of special sense; its ramifications in the retina are numerous and closely set. Nerve-corpuscles occur in that part along with the fibres, to increase the susceptibility to disturbance under a slight shock.

While in the more intellectual senses—Sight, Hearing, and Touch—the nerves have their protecting and isolating sheaths corresponding with the distinctness and separateness of the parts of the impression; in Smell, the nerves are a plexus of unsheathed fibres, corresponding with the fusion of the odorous impression into one whole, without distinction of parts (Spencer).

It has been pointed out by Mr. Spencer that to increase the delicacy of Sight and Hearing, where the impulse on the surface is very feeble, there are "multipliers of disturbance," or means of exaggerating the intensity of the shock. Thus, in the Eye, the retina is composed of ultimate fibrils unprotected by their medullary sheath, and of nerve-corpuscles, which are more unstable than the substance of the fibres. In the Ear, the little sand granules (otolites) and the rods, by being set in motion increase the action on the nerve of hearing.

The dark pigment of the eye, seen through the pupil as

a deep brown shade, is an essential of good vision, being a means of intensifying the action of the light. Attention has been drawn by Dr. Wm. Ogle to the fact, that pigment occurs also in the olfactory regions, and he traces to this fact an increase in the acuteness of smell. Dr. Ogle attributes the acuteness of the smell of the negroes, to their greater abundance of pigment. Albinos and white animals neither see nor smell so delicately as creatures that are dark-coloured. In the membranous labyrinth of the ear also, black pigment is found. ("Anosmia," by Dr. William Ogle, *Medico-Chirurgical Transactions*, vol. liii.)

Facts such as these show how deeply the mental character may be affected by the structure of the material organs. A small difference in the pigment of a sense, by giving that sense greater susceptibility, may determine the animal's preferences, tastes, and pursuits; in other words, its whole destiny. In a human being, the circumstance of being acutely sensitive in one or two leading senses, may rule the entire character—intellectual and moral. The contrast between a sensuous and a reflective nature might take its rise in the outworks of the sense organs, apart even from the endowments of the brain. In this case the nervous system would follow the cue, instead of taking the lead, of the special senses.

Next, as to correspondences between mind and body, in respect to their mode of action. Notwithstanding the

extreme difference of the two kinds of activity, bodily
and mental, we may yet find points of coincidence.

One remarkable coincidence is as respects *Time*.

By a series of very ingenious and conclusive experiments, the rate of passage of the nerve-force has been
shown to be about ninety feet per second.   This measure
is made upon the course of the nerve-threads, and does
not include the passage through the grey matter of the
centres, with their mass of corpuscles.   Now the time of
a complete circuit of action, beginning at a stimulation of
the senses, and ending in certain movements, depends
partly on the time of moving along the nerves, and partly
on the time of passing through the centres, where a
number of corpuscles must be traversed.   Estimates have
been made as to this last operation, which, from the nature
of the case, is likely to be somewhat various ; for not only
may the central mass to be penetrated be of various
extent, but also there is a liability to conflicting currents.
The case of least internal delay is what is termed *reflex
action*, where a motion answers to a stimulus, without the
intervention of the will, as in the involuntary start from a
pinch in the hand.   By experiments on frogs, Helmholtz
found that a period of from $\frac{1}{5}$ to $\frac{1}{7}$ of a second was
occupied by the reflex act ; now the length of the entire
nerve-tract could only be a few inches, which would hardly
occupy the two-hundredth of a second, if that tract were
an uninterrupted nerve-thread.

The time occupied by a sensation and subsequent volition has been measured in circumstances where there were no conflicting impulses. This is done by ascertaining the time elapsing between the sensation of a signal, and the answering by the hand. A comparison is made between two situations; one where the person is prepared beforehand, by knowing where he is to be affected and what part is to move, in which case the attention is turned upon the proper points. The other situation is where a person does not know which part is to be struck, and which part is to be moved; in this last case he has to exercise an act of judgment or consideration, and the difference of time is about the $\frac{1}{17}$th of a second. Two persons are separated by a screen; one is to utter a syllable and the other to repeat it as soon as possible. If the syllable has been agreed upon, the interval of repetition occupies from one sixth to one fourth of a second; if it is not agreed upon, the interval is one twelfth of a second more.

The example is put by M. Du Bois Raymond of a whale, ninety feet long, struck in the tail by a harpoon; one second would be occupied in transmitting the impression to the brain; a fraction of a second, say one tenth, in traversing the brain; a full second in returning the motor impulse; so that the boat would have upwards of two seconds for escaping the danger.

Thus we have physiological evidence on the one hand, that a certain time is occupied by the nerve-force, and we have mental evidence on the other, that an equivalent time is occupied by sensation, thought, and volition. Our thinking can never transcend the physical pace of the nerve-force. Seldom do we think so rapidly as the nerve-force can move; the reason is that we have so often to balance opposing considerations; in other words, opposing streams of nervous influence come together, and keep one another in suspense for a longer or shorter time. The experiments above quoted show the minimum time of a mental decision.

Another correspondence related to Time is the period required to produce a feeling or emotion. An appreciable interval must be allowed for the operation of any stimulus, in order that an appreciable feeling may be awakened—in order that we may be distinctly made conscious of a state of feeling. To become possessed of a sweet taste, some time must be allowed after the first contact with the nerve. Now this is in harmony with our legitimate inferences as to the nature of the nerve-force; the molecular changes in the nerve-centres, which accompany states of feeling, occupy an appreciable interval of time. Farther, a sensation does not decay at once, when the object is withdrawn; nor does the molecular activity set up in the centres subside at once, when the nervous prompting ceases.

It is a safe conclusion, from our knowledge of molecular forces, that the molecular changes taking place in the nerves and the nerve-centres make an alteration of substance that soon reaches a limit, incapacitating the nerves for farther change, until, by rest and assimilation, there has been a renewal of the old condition. Now to this there is an exact counterpart in our conscious experience; every sensation or emotion is most lively when first excited, becomes fainter after a time, and at last is so completely worn out that the continuation of the stimulus has no effect. The apparent exceptions, and the variations of degree, prove the rule. One of the conditions of greater persistence in any feeling is long previous remission; during a protracted interval of inaction the nerves and centres have been reinforced to a more than ordinary degree by the constant presence of nourishment, while no expenditure has been demanded.

In the employment of external agents, as warmth and food, all will admit that the sensation rises exactly as the stimulant rises, until a point is reached, when the agency changes its character, too great heat destroying the tissues, and too much food impeding digestion. There is, although we cannot fix it with numerical precision, a *sensational equivalent* of heat, of food, of muscular exercise, of sound, of light; there is a definite change of feeling, a uniform accession of pleasure or of pain, corresponding to an elevation of temperature of 10°, 20°, or 30°. So for each set of circumstances, there is a sensational equivalent of alcohol, of odours, of music, of spectacle.

It is this definite relation between outward agents and the human feelings that renders it possible to discuss human interests from the objective side, which is alone

accessible. We cannot read the feelings of our fellows ; we
merely presume that like agents will affect them all in
nearly the same way. It is thus that we measure men's
fortunes and felicity by the numerical amount of certain
agents, as money, and by the absence or low degree of
certain other agents, the causes of pain and the depressors
of vitality. And although the estimate is somewhat
rough, this is not owing to the indefiniteness of the sensational equivalent, but to the complications of the human
system, and chiefly to the narrowness of the line that
divides the wholesome from the unwholesome degrees
of all stimulants.

The simplest term that we can employ for a mental
state is a *shock* ; a word equally applicable to the bodily
side and to the mental side. A sudden stimulation of the
eye, the ear, the skin, the nose, is called a shock, from
its mere outward or physical aspect ; it is also called a
shock mentally, not because the mental consciousness resembles a material thing operating on a surface of sense,
as a ringing bell, but because there is a rapid transition
from quiescence to excitement ; in which circumstance
there is an accurate parallelism between the otherwise
distinct physical and mental facts.

The special modes of our sensations show many curious
correspondences of the physical and the mental. I select
the more prominent. In the first place, let us reflect upon
the ordinary experience of disease, into which mental

symptoms enter as a regular concomitant. There are
certain tissues that, from deficiency of nerves, are but
little sensitive, as the bones, nails, hairs, &c. ; there being
a gradation in this respect according to the extent of
connection with the brain. Now, when any derangement
operates upon the brain, directly or indirectly, the physician
looks for definite corresponding mental symptoms. The
state of the mind is dictated by the state of the brain. As
an example, note the mental symptoms of typhus fever,
summed up in the phrase "febrile oppression." "There is
great inaptitude for the exertion of the power of thought,
or of motion. The expression of the face is dull and
heavy, absent, puzzled ; the patient has the appearance of
a person made stupid by drink, &c." In short, the mind
is completely at the mercy of the bodily condition; there
is no trace of a separate, independent, self-supporting,
spiritual agent, rising above all the fluctuations of the corporeal frame. The medical practitioner assumes that to
every mental change there corresponds a physical change ;
he is, to this extent, a materialist.

There is an interesting correspondence between the
physical and the mental, in regard to a marked distinction
among the sensations, in all the senses, between the *acute*
and the *voluminous* or massive. A sharp prick in the
finger, or a hot cinder, yields acute sensations ; the contact
of the clothing of the entire body, or a warm bath, yields
voluminous or massive sensations. Now it is observable

that an acute sensation is due to an intense stimulus on
a small surface; a massive sensation to a gentler stimulus
over an extended surface. The contrast is noticeable in
every one of the senses. A gas-flame gives an acute
feeling; the diffused sunlight gives a massive feeling.
A high note upon the flageolet is acute; a deep bass note
on the violoncello or the organ is massive. The sea, the
thunder, the shouting of a multitude are voluminous or
massive from repetition over a wide area. Taste is acute,
digestive feeling is massive. Thus thoroughly does the
mere manner of external incidence determine one of the
most notable distinctions among our states of feeling.

CHAPTER IV.

GENERAL LAWS OF ALLIANCE OF MIND AND BODY.*

WE shall now give an account of the most general laws of connexion of Mind and Body. This is a difficult subject, and far from being mature; yet enough is known to gratify curiosity, and to impart useful lessons.

We have already seen grounds to believe that for every mental shock, every awakening of consciousness, every mental transition, there must be a concomitant nervous shock; and as the one is more or less intense so must be the other. Such is the most general circumstance that we are able to assign regarding the connexion. Although a very important point to establish, yet this is too vague to satisfy us.

Mind is now generally admitted to have a three-fold aspect,—three different functions—expressed by FEELING (including Emotion), WILL or Volition, and THOUGHT or Intellect. These are a trinity in unity; they are characteristic in their several manifestations, yet so dependent

* Of three papers contributed to the Fortnightly Review, in 1865, two were occupied in bringing forward the chief views here advocated respecting the physical side of the Feelings, the Will, and the Intellect; and a third contained a Historical Sketch of the Theories of the Soul, of which the last chapter is an expansion.

among themselves, that no one could subsist alone; neither
Will nor Intellect could be present in the absence of Feeling; and Feeling manifested in its completeness carries
with it the germs of the two others. Hence, although, in
tracing out the bodily accompaniments of mind, we shall
view the three powers in separation, we may expect to find
certain great laws prevailing the whole.

THE FEELINGS.

WE all know pleasure and pain, and we are familiar with
states of excitement that are neutral or indifferent.
When Feeling is opposed to Will and to Thought, it is
most characteristically represented by pleasures and pains;
these are never confounded with Thought, and although
they are motives to the Will, they do not make up the
Will. But there are many occasions when we are Excited,
roused, or rendered conscious, without being exactly pleased
or pained: and when we are not properly either willing or
thinking. Such is a mere shock of surprise; such also
are the excitements that often accompany the waning
of our proper pleasurable and painful states. After the
pain of a fright has passed away, there remains a state
of Feeling, as neutral excitement. Now there are laws
common to Feelings generally; and laws referring to
pleasures and pains particularly.

Next to the vague statement that every mental shock
is accompanied by a corresponding nervous shock, is the

law that assigns a physical counterpart to the most fundamental and general attribute of the mind, commonly termed the law or principle of Relativity.

LAW OF RELATIVITY.
(Applies both to Feeling and to Thought.)

CHANGE of impression is necessary to our being conscious.

First, on the MENTAL Side :—

It is a familiar observation that an unvarying action on any of our senses has, when long continued, the same effect as no action at all. We are not conscious of the pressure of the atmosphere. An even temperature, such as that enjoyed by the fishes in the tropical seas, leaves the mind an entire blank as regards heat and cold. The feeling of warmth is not an absolute, independent, or self-sustaining condition of mind, but the result of a transition from cold ; the sensation of light supposes a transition from darkness or shade, or from a less degree of illumination to a greater. To use a familiar illustration, a watchmaker is not conscious of the unintermitted ticking of his clocks ; but were they all suddenly stopped, he would at once become aware of the blank.

We should be astonished if a law so pervading had not been frequently remarked and expressed in literature. It has been recognized many times in forms more or less definite. One of the most definite expressions of the law was given long ago by Hobbes—" It is almost " (he should have said *altogether*) "all one for a man to be always

sensible of one and the same thing, and not to be sensible
at all of anything."

The principle has been recognized more fully in its
application to the emotions. People are generally aware
that the first shock of transition from sickness to health,
from poverty to abundance, from ignorance to insight,
is the most intense; and that, as the memory of the
previous condition fades away, so does the liveliness
of the enjoyment of the change. Shakespeare speaks
of the miser's looking but rarely at his hoards for fear of
"blunting the fine point of seldom pleasure;" and makes
the versatile Prince Hal say that—

> If all the year were playing holidays,
> To sport would be as tedious as to work.

The blessings of leisure, retirement, and rest, are pleasant
only by contrast to previous toil and excitement. The
incessant demand for novelty and change, for constant
advances in wealth, in knowledge, in the arrangements
of things about us,—attest the existence and the power
of the law of Relativity in all the provisions for enjoyment. It is a law that greatly neutralizes one part of the
advantages of superior fortune, the sense of the superiority
itself; but leaves another part untouched, namely, the
range, variety, and alternation of pleasures.

It is beyond my present limits to show how the principle
of Relativity appears in all the Fine Arts under the name
of Contrast, how it necessitates that in science and in

every kind of knowledge there should be a real negative to every real notion or real proposition ; straight—curved; motion—rest ; mind—extended matter or extended space ; how, in short, knowledge is never single but always double or two-sided, though the two sides are not always both stated. I must be content with this very brief illustration of the principle itself, and now advert to the physical counterpart.

Secondly, on the PHYSICAL side.

The chief point here is, to conceive by what arrangement of the material organization a continued agency ceases to produce that amount and kind of nervous action requisite for consciousness.

One fact of the nervous action has already been noticed. The nerve-fibres and corpuscles, on being stimulated, undergo a process of change, whereby their power is gradually exhausted ; in consequence of which they need remission and repose. Hence, the first moments of a stimulus are always the freshest, and give birth to the most vivid degrees of consciousness. This is the condition more especially requisite for maintaining a state of pleasurable sensibility. The nervous system should be duly refreshed or invigorated by nourishment and repose, and never pushed in any part to the extreme limits of exhaustion. The same condition applies to our power of active energy in every department, whether intellectual, voluntary, or emotional. Power is at the maximum, under a fresh start of renovated nerves, and fails as we approach the point of exhaustion. There are certain exceptional manifestations, as in the common experience of "growing warm" to one's work; the maximum of energy usually shows itself some time after commencing: an effect due entirely to the increased supply of blood following on a certain amount of exercise.

This fact is of the highest practical importance, and corresponds to some of our experiences in connection with the law of Relativity or Change of Impression; but it does not amount to the full significance of that law. Two circumstances still remain to be accounted for.

In the first place, the dependence of intensity of consciousness on *the degree of the transition*—as when in passing from one temperature, or one shade of light to another—is the most precise and characteristic feature of the Law of Relativity. Now, the degree of transition is connected with the degree of disturbance of the nervous currents, whether it be the quickening of the nerves from a dormant condition, or the alteration of a settled pace, to which the system has accommodated itself.

Two views may be taken of the physical adjuncts of the state of unconsciousness, the state opposed to mental wakefulness. Either the nervous mass as a whole is quiescent, that is, unagitated by currents of nervous energy, which might be supposed to be the condition of profound slumber; or currents are still kept up, but at an

even, settled, unaltering pace.   There are facts and
analogies in favour of both views.   The mode of stating
the ultimate physical condition of all consciousness depends
upon how we decide between the two suppositions.

As regards the first, it would seem natural to suppose
that the nerves pass from the state of perfect repose to
a state of greater or less activity or excitement, according
as they are roused by stimulation, and that we are made
conscious accordingly; while the remission of the stimulus, and their own exhaustion, tend to quiescence and
to unconsciousness.   If we had no facts pointing to a
different conclusion, we should adopt this as the most
conformable to all analogy.   But there are facts pointing
the other way.   The nervous system is rarely allowed
to fall into entire somnolence.   In profound sleep, the
reflex actions go on; these, however, we may disregard,
as having detached themselves from the conscious circles.
Still, although when awake, we keep up activity more
or less, and are under the stimulation of several senses, yet
we often become almost unconscious of either the activity
or the sensations; the only thing necessary for this
result is that these shall be for the time monotonous
or invariable.   The most likely interpretation to be put
upon so familiar an experience would seem to be that there
are *always* currents of nerve-force, but that consciousness
disappears according as these are unvaried in their degree.
Many of the best established facts of the system are in
favour of a certain low degree of nerve action as existing

E

under every variety of state ; such, for example, as the muscular tension maintained in the most perfect sleep.

On this hypothesis our conception is, that when all the currents of the brain are equally balanced, and continue at the same pitch—when no one is commencing, increasing or abating—consciousness or feeling is null, mind is quiescent. A *disturbance* of this state of things wakens up the consciousness for a time ; *another* disturbance gives it another fillip, and so on ; the variety of stimulus in the waking state forbidding the perfect equilibrium from being attained. In harmony with this supposition is the really fitful nature of the mind ; the stream of consciousness is a series of ebullitions rather than a calm or steady flow. The calmness that we actually experience belongs to a low or moderate excitement ; let there be any considerable intensity of feeling, and the ebullition character will start out convincingly prominent.

In the present state of our knowledge, no certain decision between the two conflicting hypotheses should be hazarded. We must wait for an *experimentum crucis*, and perhaps the real state of the case is not accurately expressed by either.

The foregoing discussion embraces the law of pure Relativity, Change, or Transition, as connected with mental wakefulness, or consciousness. But in the concrete examples of the mental fact as above expressed, there is a farther circumstance not involved in what has now been brought out. We have made allowance for the decay of an impression after a certain continuance; leaving still the possibility that, after a suitable remission or interruption, the impression may be renewed in all its fulness.

But now, among the features of those experiences given from the mental side of Relativity, this stands out prominent, namely, that no *second occurrence* of any great shock or stimulus, whether pleasure, pain, or mere excitement, is ever fully equal to the first, notwithstanding that full time has been given for the nerves to recover from their exhaustion. There is a certain amount of decay in the force of every impression, on the after-occasions when it is revived. Such is the statement of the law of Novelty, with which we are all familiar.

In all probability, we have here only a new and more complicated phase of the law of Transition. We need to suppose that the system accommodates itself to every new state of things, that a permanent trace is made (through the operation of the retentive power), and that under a fresh shock this accommodation operates by diminishing the interval of transition, the difference between the present impression and the pre-established attitudes and arrangements of the nervous system.

It is needless to push this speculation beyond a general surmise. Until a more precise expression can be given to the modes of the nervous action under the single circumstance of mere transition, permanent accommodation being left out of account, we cannot hope to deal with the com-

plication of two circumstances. Still, a reasonable probability attaches to the hypotheses of physical action that
have now been suggested.

LAW OF DIFFUSION.

When an impression is accompanied with Feeling, the
aroused currents *diffuse* themselves freely over the brain,
leading to a general agitation of the moving organs, as
well as affecting the viscera.

Illustrative Contrast.—The so-called reflex actions
(breathing, swallowing, &c.) are commonly said to have
no feeling; at the same time, they are accomplished in
a limited circuit or channel.

Note of Explanation.—It is not meant that every
fibre and cell can be affected at one moment, but that a
spreading wave is produced sufficient to agitate the body
at large.

We have seen generally what it is that nervous action
consists in. A stimulus on a sensitive surface affects a
sensitive nerve. It thence proceeds to some ganglionic
centre, there liberating a still more energetic force, which
passes by motor nerves to muscles. The completed fact
of a nervous shock is a muscular movement. But, owing
to the numerous cross connexions that make up the
aggregate of corpuscles, or the grey central matter, the
sensory stimulus proceeds first to one corpuscle, and then
is diffused to others successively, until it affects a great
many, before it reaches motor nerves; and when these

are reached they are so numerous as to actuate a wide
circle of movements. Now it is found that consciousness
or feeling increases with the extent of the wave, or the
number of the central corpuscles excited, and the consequent number of outward movements commenced.
Feeling is only nascent in the case of a simple sensory
stimulus, one passing through a limited group of corpuscles,
and producing a simple movement. We cannot say that
even then consciousness or feeling is absolutely non-
existent; but it begins to be decisively manifest when
the wave spreads right and left, by the corpuscular
crossings; and it grows with the extension of this wave.
We assume, as a fundamental fact, that, with nervous
action, feeling begins. We cannot draw a line between
nervous action without feeling, and nervous action with
feeling; we can only indicate a scale of degree. Yet, to
all intents and purposes, there is a division of nervous
actions into unconscious and conscious, which is illustrative
of the general law of Diffusion.

The reflex actions,—breathing, the movements of the
intestines, the heart's action, winking, &c.,—are known to
be stimulated through the spinal cord, and its immediate
continuations at the base of the brain; they do not
involve the cerebral mass. The responding movements in
the case of each of them are limited to the work to be
done; to the chest, in breathing; to the intestines, in
propelling the food; to the muscles of the heart, in

pumping the blood.   These actions are unaccompanied
with feeling.   So, in touching the hand of one asleep,
we see the hand curl up, or the arm move away.   This
is called reflex ; it is prompted through the lower centres,
without lateral diffusion or communication, and it is
directed to a single local group of muscles.   In such
examples, as formerly seen, the limitation is owing to
want of force.   There are ways open to the brain;
but they are not entered at the instance of a · very
feeble contact.   Still, the fact of limitation of range
is accompanied by the fact of unconsciousness : an
isolated response is our evidence for contraction of the
sphere of excitement ; and such isolated responses are
little, if at all, accompanied with feeling.

Compare now what happens in a shock, say of acute pain,
as from a severe smart or a wound in the same part, namely,
the hand.   A reflex influence would still operate, and give
birth to movements of the arm ; but these would be a small
part of the case.   The bodily members everywhere are put
in motion ; the features are contracted with a well-known
expression ; the voice sends out a sharp cry ; the whole
body is thrown into agitation.   Nor do the effects stop
with mere muscular movements ; the face is flushed,
showing that the circulation is disturbed ; the breathing is
quickened, or the reverse; a temporary loss of appetite
proves that the gastric secretions in the stomach are per-
verted ; the skin is deranged ; and in the feminine constitution it would appear as if the mother's milk were

turned into gall. In order to cause this wide circle
of effects, the influence of the shock, the nerve-currents
set on, must be not merely intense in degree, but
highly diffused in their course through the brain; being
thus able to reach and to actuate the general system of
out-carrying nerves.

I have taken an extreme case to present the law in its
utmost prominence. We might vary the illustration, and
show that according to the strength of a feeling is *the
extent of the diffusion*, as well as the intensity of the
diffused manifestations. The rise and fall of these two
facts, in steady concomitance, is among our most common
experiences; indeed, our principal means of interpreting
the strength of one another's feelings is derived from this
uniformity. It would also be easy to prove that the
apparent exceptions to the law are not real exceptions;
that in very mild states of feeling, or under a faint degree
of excitement, the diffused wave is not strong enough to
excite the muscles to an open display; that the will may
suppress the display; that habit may suppress it;
that, when the system is so strongly pre-engaged by another influence as to resist a new diffusion, impressions
are not felt (as in the insensibility to wounds in a
battle).

I will not dwell on these illustrations, and will merely
add a reference to the operation of habit in deadening
the feeling that accompanies our actions, to show that,

wherever this deadening influence has occurred, the diffused wave is proportionably contracted and suppressed. In our first attempts to write, to cipher, to play on an instrument, to speak, or in any other work of mechanical skill,—the inward sense of labour and difficulty is corresponded to by the number of awkward and irrelevant gesticulations. On the other hand, in the last stage of consummated facility and routine, the consciousness is almost nothing; and the general quietude of the body demonstrates that the course of power has now become narrowed to the one channel necessary for the exact movements required. This is a sort of educated imitation of the primitive reflex movement adduced at the outset; the comparison is so striking as to suggest to physiologists the designation of secondary reflex or automatic, for the habitual movements. A man at a signal post, after long habit, is subjected to little or no nervous influence, except in the single thread of connection between a certain figure depicted on the eye and a certain movement of the hand; the collaterals of the primitive wave have died away, and the accompanying consciousness has fallen to a barely discernible trace.

The law of Diffusion might be called in to confirm the hypothetical account of the process of accommodation adverted to under Relativity. The failing intensity of renewed impressions might be connected with a narrower and weaker diffusion. Now, our study of the physical basis of Retentiveness (see Chap. V.) shows the tendency of all nervous states, by repetition, to narrow their compass of action, and to run into special channels of connexion with the states that happen to succeed them; substituting intellectual trains for emotional outbursts.

It is by combining the two laws—Relativity and Diffusion—that we obtain the comprehensive statement of the physical conditions of all consciousness :—*An increase or variation of the nerve-currents of the brain sufficiently energetic and diffused to affect the combined system of the out-carrying nerves (both motor nerves and nerves of the viscera).*

To all the varieties of human feeling, there correspond (we must suppose) varieties of diffusion in the brain, as there correspond, to a very considerable extent, varieties in the external manifestation. The outward signs are only a small part of the wave of effects upon muscles and viscera; many movements receive a mere incipient stimulus, too weak for producing action (not to speak of counter-impulses of suppression), and most of the visceral alterations fail to show themselves to the observer. The diffused wave of nervous energy is an inseparable adjunct of feeling. The consequent manifestations of movement and gesture are the universal language of feeling, and possess a constancy that, among all the variations of human character, is truly remarkable. This is what I previously put forward as the first argument for the thorough connexion of mind and body; the region of facts

most open to vulgar observation, and yet most persis-
tently overlooked by the supporters of the dissociation or
independence of mind and matter.

The varieties of Expression of the feelings constitute a
study of great interest as regards our present theme ; but
it will be enough to advert, under the following head, to
the one broad and characteristic distinction of pleasure and
pain.

LAWS OF PLEASURE AND PAIN.

Pleasure and Pain have certain well known agents or
causes, and they have also a characteristically distinct
outcome of demeanour and expression. It is an interesting,
although not very easy, problem to sum these up in a
general law, or laws, of concomitance of mind and body.
The principle that regulates feeling in general is liable to
considerable modification according as the feeling assumes
the character of either pleasure or pain.

As a preliminary remark, it must be allowed that
pleasure and pain are diametrically opposed, like cold and
heat, up and down, debt and credit, plus and minus. The
two are mutually destructive, they neutralize each other,
like cold and heat. Hence the circumstances present in
connexion with the one must be absent, if not reversed,
in the case of the other ; whatever mode of nervous
excitement is allied with pain, its opposite must be
allied with pleasure. Thus one explanation should
nclude both.

Law of Self-Conservation.

The remark has occurred to various speculators that there is a close connexion between Pleasure and high vitality, or the vigour of the system, and between Pain and the causes of diminished vitality, or the feebleneass and exhaustion of the system. Plato and Aristotle, in their views regarding Pleasure, included its being a restorative to nature. Kant has a few striking expressions of the same tendency, although their effect is greatly spoiled by the context :—" Pleasure is the feeling of the furtherance, Pain of the hindrance of life." A very large number of the facts may be included in the following statement, which may be termed the Law of Self-Conservation :—

States of Pleasure are connected with an increase, states of Pain with an abatement, of some or all of the vital functions.

This principle resumes such well known experiences as these :—The pleasures of healthy exercise, and of rest after toil, the pain of fatigue ; the pleasures of nourishment and pure air, the pains of hunger, inanition, or suffocation ; the pleasures of health generally, the pains of bodily injury and disease. These few instances sum up the ruling facts of every one's daily life and bodily and mental condition.

There are, however, a few startling exceptions For example :—Cold may be painful and yet wholesome, as in the cold bath, and under the keen bracing air. But this exception, on closer view, confirms the general rule, while rendering its application more definite. Cold undoubtedly depresses, for a time, one very sensitive organ, the Skin, perhaps also the Digestive Organs ; while, in moderate degree (that is, the degree constituting wholesomeness) it exalts, through the capillary circulation, the lungs, the heart, the muscles, and the nerves ; and the contrast teaches us that, as far as *immediate pleasure* is concerned, we lose more by depressing the functions of the skin and the stomach, than we gain by increasing the power of the heart, the lungs, the muscles, or even the nerves themselves.

Another very remarkable exception is the painlessness of many diseases, together with the occasional absence of all pain, and even the presence of great comfort, in the sick bed and in the final decay of life. This is the case so often pointed to as evincing the triumph of the mind over the body.

The remark already made in the case of cold, must be still farther extended to meet this case. The connexion of pleasure with vitality, and of pain with feebleness or loss of function, does not apply to all organs alike ; some are comparatively insensitive, their degeneracy and decay seem unaccompanied with feeling ; while in others the smallest functional derangement is productive of pain. Muscular weakness does not give pain, unless we are compelled to efforts beyond our strength ; also the nervous system may be enfeebled as regards thinking power without producing discomfort, provided we are allowed perfect repose. On the other hand, anything that impairs nutrition, as indigestion, leads to immediate discomfort; and still more decided is any partial stoppage of the purifying organs, as the intestines, the liver, the skin, the lungs, or the kidneys. There are forms of degeneration of the heart, the lungs, the kidneys, and other parts, that do not interfere with the usual functions; their evil consists in preparing the way for a sudden break-down.

The powers of the nervous system are various and even mutually opposed. Intellectual feebleness, decay of memory, and incapability of thought, are not painful in themselves. There is, probably, a distinct power of the nervous system, connected with the pleasurable tone of the mind, which may not fail, when the intellect fails, or may fail, while the intellect is yet vigorous; a function very unequally manifested in different individuals.

The mental effect of diminished power in the various organic functions is ultimately realized by some failure in the brain itself. Could we suppose the brain to maintain all its functions, derangement might exist in other organs without depressing the mind. Strictly speaking, this is an impossible concurrence. But there is sometimes an approach to this situation, namely, when the blood, such as it is, flows in excess to the brain, supporting its powers at the expense of all other interests; an arrangement that cannot be permanent, although it may last for a little time. In such a contingency there is an extraordinary exaltation of mental function, including a hilarious and even ecstatic enjoyment. It is the state that narcotics may produce, for a brief moment, in a constitution partially wrecked; and it occasionally occurs in the closing hours of life. We often see patients in the last stage of consumption, still entertaining the most sanguine prospects of recovery; a proof that, instead of being mentally depressed, they are in the opposite or joyous condition. On this it is remarked by Dr. Patrick Nicol (Medical Reports of West Riding Asylum for 1872, p. 199) "that blood, from which tubercle is deposited, appears to have that peculiar injurious property for the brain *which excites delirium* ;" in extreme cases, it is productive of raving madness.

The general principle, connecting pleasure with increase of vital power, receives farther confirmation from the outward displays under pleasure and pain; the animation, stir, and vigour under the one, and the drooping and collapse under the other.

The primary law of feeling, that movement is in proportion to intensity of stimulation, is greatly modified according as the feeling is pleasurable or painful. Mere intensity of stimulus operates to give intensity of movement; but the character of the feeling as pleasure, as pain or as neutral excitement, must also be taken into account. The designations for pleasure are very significant of the

difference : the epithets—lively, animated, gay, cheerful,
hilarious—are expressive of unusual activity; the epithets—
sad, miserable, woe-begone, depressed, sorrowful, dejected,
crest-fallen,—suggest languor, prostration, inactivity. With
the young, we see in especial prominence the union of the
two facts—mental delight and bodily energy. The examination of the organic functions conclusively shows that in
a pleasurable mood these are raised in efficiency ; the respiration is quicker, the pulse is better, the digestive functions are exalted.   In depression and pain, all is reversed.

An apparent exception to the law occurs in the stimulating effects of an acute smart, and in the contortions
and struggling of pain generally. This, however, is no real
exception, as the following considerations will show.

In the first place, many painful shocks are simply
and solely depressing ; they have not even the pretence
or appearance of rousing the energies. A blow on the
shin is utterly prostrating ; the irritation of a raw wound
has much the same effect. Certain parts of the body, on
being squeezed, compressed, or tortured, yield an intense
pain that at once quenches all the energies. Cold, in its
painful forms, excepting, perhaps, the contact with a small
congealed surface, which resembles a scald, is mainly
depressing ; when it re-acts to exalt the functions, its
painful character disappears. Privation, calamity, sever-
ance of ties, shame, remorse, are accompanied with general
prostration of the energies.

In the next place, the vehement muscular stimulation due to acute pains can be shown to be accompanied with loss of power in the organic functions; it is thus a mere spasmodic display, the result of a spendthrift energy. The stomach, the heart, the lungs, are all depressed, to support a wasteful exertion of muscle.

That the exertion is forced and factitious is farther proved by the lassitude that succeeds; the muscles themselves show an exhaustion very different from what would follow on a similar amount of healthy exertion, or in the excitement of joy.*

Still, an acute smart is one mode of temporarily raising the energies; the acuteness implying that the pain is limited to a very small circle of nerves, so that the injurious effects are confined, while the stimulus suffices to arouse a wave of force-bearing nerve-currents. The light smart of a horse-whip is enough to waken the energies, without damaging the vitality. The pain of a flogging, which multiplies smarts of still greater intensity, is utterly exhausting to the whole system.

* There have occurred many instances of death, or mental derangement, from a shock of grief, pain, or calamity; this is in accordance with the general law. Instances are also recorded of death and insanity from excessive joy; but they are so rare as to have the character of exceptions. Extreme intensity of shock, whatever be its character, is unhinging; but there is a wide difference in the consequences, according as it is the intensity of pain or the intensity of pleasure. From the one shock, people, as a rule, recover slowly and with difficulty; from the other, they recover rapidly and easily.

In this law of Pleasure and Pain, we have the key to the leading varieties of Expression of the Feelings. The organs of expression by movement are primarily the features, next the voice, lastly the movements and gestures of the body at large—head, trunk, and extremities. In pleasurable emotions, these are unquestionably rendered active; the grimaces, gestures, and attitudes, show an accession of active power. The notable circumstances in this display are the general erection of the body, the opening up of the features, the powerful exercise of the voice; all showing that the extensor muscles, which are by far the largest, are strongly stimulated. When we have surplus energy to expend, we stretch and extend the body in preference to bending and relaxing it; the weight of the body itself is borne in the one case and not in the other. Any additional strain, as in walking, lifting weights, rowing a boat, is borne by the extensor muscles. It is the size of these that makes the muscular figure, the fulness of the calves, the thighs, and the hips.

On the other hand, pain (not violently acute), dejection, depression, leads to the relaxation of all these powerful muscles; hence a general stooping and collapse of the figure, showing that the springs of muscular force have dried up. The difference of the two situations, as regards the carriage of the whole body, is most marked. Compare the victor in a triumph with one of his captives—the attitude of the beater with the beaten. And as regards

F

the face, how much is suggested by the one descriptive trait—"his countenance fell"!

To this general law we find a remarkable exception that puzzled the great physiologist, Müller of Berlin, and was left unsolved by Sir Charles Bell. It refers to the expression of the Face. While the movements under pleasure are obvious and energetic—the raising of the eye-brows, the drawing outwards of the angles of the mouth; there are also some apparently energetic movements characteristic of pain—the lowering of the eye-brows, the wrinkling the forehead, the drawing down of the angle of the mouth, the pouting of the lower lip. Now, to have one set of muscles acting strongly under pleasure, and another set acting strongly under pain, would merely be two modes of activity; it would not represent opposition or contrariety. Yet pleasure and pain are as opposite as heat and cold. What causes the one arrests or destroys the other; and no theory of the physical accompaniments is complete that fails to bring out this contrariety. It would be a self-contradictory account of solvency and insolvency, to say that one was property in the funds, and the other property in land; and there is an equal contradiction in having muscles of pleasure and muscles of pain.

One way of diminishing the difficulty is to carry out a little farther the foregoing contrast of the attitudes in pleasure and in pain — the one erect the other collapsed. In addition to remitting the powerful exertion of extending the body, one might suppose the flexor muscles exerted to make it still more thoroughly collapse, to distend to the utmost the strong erecting muscles. Now, one effect of this would be to release the muscular currents, and to set free the blood and the nerve-force in favour of the other interests of the system,—Digestion, &c., which are the first to suffer in great pain or in dejection of mind. The cost of the flexor effort is but small, and the return in the liberation of the nervous and muscular currents might more than compensate for that cost. The contrariety of the two states would be saved, while there would still be an active prompting under pain.

Applying this explanation to the Face, we should have to consider whether the muscular opposition in it could show, in the one case, the exertion of powerful muscles, and in the other, their relaxation by the operation of those of smaller calibre. A slight exertion of the small muscle that corrugates the eye-brows, may be supposed to perfect the relaxation of the more powerful muscle of the scalp that raises the eye-brows; a small stream of energy in the muscle surrounding the mouth relaxes more thoroughly the strong zygomatic muscles, and the buccinator, which are distended in smiling and laughter. By the employment of a slight force, we may be supposed to release a greater quantity; so that, after all, the positive exertion of those specific muscles of pain would merely aid in renouncing muscular energy on the whole. We should thus assign as the reason why a forced " sadness of the coun-

tenance makes the heart better," that, by the employment
of a certain amount of stimulus, we more thoroughly abate
the stimulation of the moving organs at large, and allow
blood and nervous force to pass to the enfeebled viscera—
the digestion, the lungs, the heart, the skin—by whose
amelioration the mental tone is decisively improved.*

* A new turn has been given to the explanation of the facial attitudes
under pleasure and pain, first by Mr. Spencer, in the new edition of his
Psychology, and next in Mr. Darwin's recent work on Expression. The
novelty lies in applying the doctrine of Evolution, or inheritance, to
account for the more special and characteristic modes of expression of
the face, as, for example, frowning, smiling, pouting, and depressing
the corners of the mouth. The same doctrine is also applied to
account for the expression of the more marked passions, as fear, love,
anger.

It does not lie within the plan of this work to discuss the details of
the human feelings, either in their internal characters, or in their outward display; nor is it my purpose to enter into the merits of the
doctrine of Evolution as applied to the mind. So far as I have here
gone, in assigning the most general laws of connexion of mind and body,
I am not at variance with any views set forth by these two great
authorities, although I have given far more prominence than either of
them to the law that connects Pleasure with an accession of vital
Power, and Pain with depressed vitality. As regards my first law—called
the law of Diffusion—both Mr. Spencer and Mr. Darwin have treated it
under different phraseology, but in substantially the same way. It is
the third of Mr. Darwin's three Laws for explaining the phenomena of
expression—termed by him the law of the "direct action of the excited
nervous system."

Mr. Darwin furnishes incidentally many striking illustrations and
confirmations of the Law of Pleasure and Pain. Among the appearances of protracted grief, he remarks—"The circulation becomes
languid; the face pale; the muscles flaccid; the eyelids droop; the
head hangs on the contracted chest; the lips, cheeks, and lower jaw all
sink downwards from their own weight." (p. 178.) Let any one
compare this with the expression of a bride and bridegroom at the
beginning of their honeymoon.

Mr. Darwin's second law, called by him the principle of Antithesis,

An examination, after Sir Charles Bell, of the two great convulsive outbursts—Laughter and Sobbing—gives an unequivocal support to the law; the one signifies in all its points the accession of vital force; the other equally signifies loss, failure, or deprivation of energy. "The whole expression of a man in good spirits is exactly the opposite of one suffering from sorrow" (Darwin, p. 213). In both cases there may be energetic displays: but while the energy of laughter leaves no sting behind, the energy of convulsive grief is succeeded by utter prostration.

The law now illustrated is named the Law of Self-conservation, because without it the system could not be maintained. Inasmuch as we follow pleasure and avoid pain, if pleasure were injurious and pain wholesome, we should soon incur entire shipwreck of our vitality, as we often partially do, through certain tendencies that are exceptional to the general law.

occasionally leads him to exemplify the opposing effects of Pleasure and Pain, as one of the various forms of Antithesis, or the tendency to pass from one expression to its opposite, even although the opposing mental state would not generate that opposed expression. The principle of Opposition has been recognized in the text under two forms—first, the fundamental law of Pleasure and Pain (Self-Conservation), and secondly, the employment of the small flexor muscles to complete the contraction of the powerful extensors, and secure a more perfect attitude of repose and renunciation of nervous stimulus.

The violent contortions of acute pain are referred by Mr. Darwin to inherited habits of exertion for getting rid of pain. He would even regard the excited movements of animals under delight as partly associations with hunting and the search for food; although he freely admits that the state of pleasure is itself accompanied with increased vigour of the circulation and the nerve-force.

Law of Stimulation or Exercise.

To stimulate or excite the nerves, with a due regard to their condition, is pleasurable ; to pass this limit, painful.

The mere presence of nourishment, that is, blood, does not evoke all the nervous activity that the blood can pay for, and the nerves maintain with safety ; the case is rather that the blood yields up force at the instance of stimulated nerve-currents.   Now this stimulation, when in the proper degree, is connected with pleasure, while there is a degree that is always painful ; both points varying with the condition of the individual.

If we commence the illustration from the side of Pain, we may notice as two leading circumstances, (1) Conflict, and (2) Intensity.

First. To say that all *conflicting* stimulations are painful, is merely to state a consequence of the former position. Conflict is waste of vital power, and is likely to be accompanied by a depression of the mental tone.   This simple and obvious maxim sums up a wide experience; it includes the pleasures of harmony and the pains of discord ; the pleasures of a free scope to all our impulses and the pains of constraint, obstruction, and thwarted aims; the pleasure of discovering similarity, agreement, consistency, and unity, the pains of inconsistency and contradiction.

Secondly. As regards *intensity*.   Violent, excessive, and sudden stimulations induce pain on various grounds.   In opposition to the law that connects pleasure with vital energy, they cause a momentary exhaustion of the power of the nerves affected ; and they may further be considered as originating a conflict with the prevailing currents of the brain, which do not adjust themselves at once to the new impetus. Thus though, on the general principle of relativity, they waken up a strong feeling, they sin against the conditions of *pleasurable* feeling.

Conflict and Violence, then, are two principal modes of painful stimulation, and explain a very considerable number of our pains. In most, if not in all, of the painful sensations of three of the senses—namely, Touch, Hearing, and Sight—the pain is either discord or excess. The smarting acuteness of a blow on the skin, of a railway whistle close to the ear, of a glare of light—are due to the mere degree or excess of the stimulus. In hearing and in sight, there are, in addition, the pains of discord. In the two remaining senses, Taste and Smell, we cannot make the same affirmation. We do not know what is the mode of nervous action in a bitter taste, as quinine or soot; and we cannot say that the transition from sweet to bitter is a transition from moderate stimulus to an excessive one. It may be that the power of the nerve is exhausted under a different kind of influence from mere violence of stimulation; but no certain knowledge exists on the subject. The same remarks apply to smell.

These observations on the *negative* aspect of stimulation

—the aspect of pain—contain by implication the positive aspect. Stimulation, as such, is pleasurable. " Man loves sensation," said Aristotle. For the eye to see, for the ear to hear, for the skin to touch, are in themselves agreeable. We cannot affirm, with respect to the ordinary gratification of the five senses, that they increase vitality —they may do so slightly; we can say only that they draw upon the vitality to maintain nerve-currents that give pleasure. It is agreeable to spend a certain portion of the forces of the system in nervous electricity; it is not agreeable to push this expenditure beyond a certain point. And when the stimulation has passed this point, degenerating into pain, the pleasurable tone can be restored only by replenishing the vital power, according to the principle that connects pleasure with vitality.

I may remark, as confirming all that has been said, what is our common experience and practice with regard to pleasure, namely, the great value of the stimulants that are not intense but *voluminous*—that moderately affect a large sensitive surface, or many nerves at once : a familiar instance is furnished by the warm bath ; another is the music of a full band. The same happy effect springs from change or variety ; the stimulation is multiplied, and no one part pushed to exhaustion.

The last point that I will advert to is the obscure sub-ject of Narcotic stimulants—alcohol, tea, tobacco, opium, and the rest. These operate a very little way, if at all, in giving new vitality; they draw upon our vitality, even till it is much below par, postponing the feeling of depression till another day. It is probable that the influence of the narcotics is complicated, and not the same for all. We may safely say respecting them, that they are the extreme instance of the principle of Stimulation, as contrasted with the principle of vital conservation ; they are the large consumers, not the producers, of vitality; they expend our stock of power in nerve-electricity in a higher degree, and with a more dangerous licence, than the ordinary stimulants of the senses.

The physical theory of Pleasure and Pain has a direct bearing on Punishment and Prison Discipline. I happened to be present at a debate on that subject, in one of the sections of the British Association, at the Manchester meeting in 1861. The speakers were bent upon suggesting modes of punishment, painfully deterring, and yet not injurious to the convict's health. I could not help remarking, from my conviction of the doctrine now expressed, that the object aimed at is all but a contradiction. There is, if any, the barest margin between the infliction of pain and the destruction of vital power. If the first of the two maxims above stated (the connexion of pleasure with vital conservation, &c.,) expressed the whole truth, there would be no margin at all; but under the second maxim (Stimulation), there might be room to operate as proposed. Stimulants cannot, as a general rule, be said to increase vital power; they are usually on the verge of destroying it, and frequently do destroy it. Consequently, the *withholding of stimulation*—alcohol, tobacco, tea, cheerful light and spectacle, the sounds of busy life, society, amusing literature, &c.—cannot be said necessarily to abate the vital forces, and may be instrumental in conserving them. Nevertheless, if these are withheld to the extent of making them strongly craved for (and, if they are not, their loss does not punish), the state of craving is an internal conflict that lowers the general vitality. If the craving dies away after a time, the depression ceases, and so does the punishment. Then, again, it might seem that the application of what is *painfully salubrious* would exactly hit the mark ; as the cold bath, the well-ventilated and but moderately-heated cell, cleanliness, measured food, steady industry, and regularity of life. Yet unless the convict takes kindly to these various measures, they are more depressing than wholesome ; and if his system does adapt itself, that is, if they end in reforming his constitution and habits, they are no longer punishment. In the debate in question, one of the speakers, who I believe was officially connected with a London prison, remarked that, as a rule, discharged convicts are deteriorated in constitution. The opposite allegation has sometimes been made ; but between the two I will venture to arbitrate by saying that, in whatever cases the confinement operates as a serious punishment, the deterioration is almost certain. The same speaker observed that corporal punishment has this advantage over imprisonment—that, while it is a severe deterring smart, it does not to the same degree inflict permanent damage. *

* The two modes of punishing by physical torture, are severe muscular strain (hard labour, the crank, tread-wheel) and flogging. The one operates upon the nerves through the muscular tissue, the other through the skin. There is no intention of injuring either the muscles or the skin in themselves ; the sole object is to produce a painful condition of the nerves. Yet, as it is hardly possible, in severe punishments, to avoid permanent damage to the intermediate tissue—muscle or skin—some plan might be devised for affecting the nerves alone. Recourse might be had to Electricity. By electrical shocks and currents, and especially by Faraday's Magneto-electric machine, which constantly breaks and renews the currents, any amount of torture might be inflicted ; and the graduation might be made with scientific precision. How far the nerves would suffer permanent injury by a severe application of electricity is still a matter for inquiry ; probably not more than by an equal amount of suffering through the muscular or skin punishments ; while, at all events, the damage would be confined to the nervous tissue. The punishment would be less revolting to the spectator and the general public than floggings, while it would not be less awful to the criminal himself ; the mystery of it would haunt the imagination, and there would be no conceivable attitude of alleviating endurance. The terrific power exercised by an operator, through the lightest finger touch, would make more deeply felt the humiliating prostration of the victim.

If capital punishments are to be permanently maintained, much could be said for discarding strangulation, and substituting an electric shock. But there being a growing opinion unfavourable to the extinction of life, as a mode of punishment, the combination of imprisonment with electric inflictions could be graduated to a severity of endurance that should satisfy all demands for retribution to offenders. It was remarked by Lord Romilly that imprisonment with periodic floggings would be far worse than immediate execution. The idea would be too painful to the community at large ; while a more refined application of pain would pass unheeded, except by the sufferer.

THE WILL.

The Will, volition, or voluntary action is, on the outside, a physical fact; animal muscle under nervous
stimulation is one of the mechanical prime movers; the
motive power of muscle is as purely physical as the
motive power of steam; food is to the one what fuel is
to the other.   The distinguishing peculiarity of our
voluntary movements is that they take their rise in
Feeling, and are guided by Intellect; hence, so far as
Will is concerned, the problem of physical and mental
concomitance is still a problem either of Feeling or of
Intellect. The extension and improvement of our voluntary
power is one large department of our education; and the
process of education is wholly included under the Intellect.
I shall confine myself, then, as regards the Will to a short
statement of the fundamental processes involved in it,
one of which has just been before us under the Feelings,
and will again appear as playing a part in the Intellect.
In the Will altogether I reckon up *three* elements; two
primitive, instinctive, or primordial, and the third a process
of education or acquirement.

The first primordial element is called the Spontaneous
Energy or Surplus Activity of the system, or the dis-
position of the moving organs to come into operation
of themselves previous to, and apart from, the stimulation
of the senses or the feelings; the activity being increased

when such stimulation concurs with the primitive spontaneity. I think there is evidence to show that the profuse activity attendant on health, nourishment, youth, and a peculiar temperament called the active temperament, springs in a very great degree from inherent active power, with no purpose at first, but merely to expend itself; and that such activity gradually comes under the guidance of the feelings and purposes of the animal. It is the surplus nervous power of the system discharging itself without waiting for the promptings of sensation. In the course of education the spontaneity is so linked with our feelings as to be an instrument of our well-being, in promoting pleasures and removing pains. The voice by mere spontaneity sends forth sounds, the ear controls and directs them into melody, and the wants of the system generally make them useful in other ways.

Mere spontaneity, however, would not give us all that we find in the impulses of the Will. Being the overflow of vital power, it would show itself only whenever and wherever there is such an overflow. We want a kind of activity that shall start forth at any time when pleasure is to be secured, or pain to be banished, and that shall be directed to the very points where these effects can be commanded.

For such a power we must refer to the great funda-

mental law of Pleasure and Pain—the law that connects
Pleasure with increase of Vital Power, Pain with
the diminution of Vital Power. This law we may look
upon as in many respects the foundation, the main-
stay, of our being ; it is the principle of self-conservation
—the self-regulating, self-acting impulse of the animal
system. When anyhow we come into a mood of joyful
elation, the physical state corresponding is an exaltation
of vital energy to the muscles, the organic functions, one
or other, or both ; and that exaltation is an increase of
the activity that is bringing the pleasure. The first act
of masticating a morsel of food develops a pleasurable
feeling to the conscious mind, and a concurrent stimulus
of heightened activity to the body; the heightened
activity vents itself in the parts actually moving at the
time—the masticating organs, the cheeks, jaw, and tongue,
which in consequence proceed with redoubled vigour, the
pleasure thus feeding itself. In that connexion we have,
as I believe, the deepest foundation of the will. On the
other hand, if, in the course of energetic movements of
mastication, a false step occurs, the teeth embracing
by mistake the skin of the lip or the tongue, there is
mentally a smart of pain, and physically, I think, a
destruction of nervous power through the shock, and the
destruction of power is at once and directly a cessation
of the active currents impelling the mouth and the jaws.

Such I conceive to be the groundwork of Volition,

greatly, but never entirely, overlaid in mature life by a large superstructure of acquired connexions between feelings and specific movements.   Without some such foundation I see no way of beginning the work of voluntary acquisition, nothing to make our movements relevant to our state of feeling at the time ; moreover, it is the check that is always ready to step in and supersede our acquired habits.   At any moment a burst of pleasure will raise our energies, a shock of pain (not being an acute exciting smart) will depress them ; in the one case the cause of the pleasure, if our over-activity, will be maintained with increase ; in the other case the energies are arrested, and if they are causing the pain, it will cease with them. The bursting out of a cheerful light in a dark labyrinth spurs us on without our going through the formality of what we call a resolution of the will ; while a course leading us to darkness, strangeness, and uncertainty will be arrested by the mere sinking away of our energies before we can even begin to deliberate.   Our course in life from first to last, although most at first, is trial and error, groping and feeling our way, acting somehow, and judging of the result ; and the general tendency of the law in question is to sustain us when we are in a good track, to turn off the steam when we are in a bad track.

CHAPTER V.

THE INTELLECT.*

I now approach the most difficult part of the subject of the physical basis of mind—namely, what regards the Intellect. That the Feelings are closely connected with physical manifestations is patent and undeniable. But Thought is at times so quiet, so far removed from bodily demonstrations, that we might suppose it conducted in a region of pure spirit, merely imparting its conclusions through a material intervention. Unfortunately for this supposition, the fact is now generally admitted, that thought exhausts the nervous substance, as surely as walking exhausts the muscles. Our physical framework is involved with thought no less decidedly than with feeling ; and it is requisite to define, if possible, the terms of the alliance.

In the positions already advanced, with respect to the

* This chapter may not perhaps be easily understood by readers unfamiliar with the theory of our Intellectual Powers. It is not essential to the general argument ; while it is more purely hypothetical and speculative than the foregoing chapter on the Feelings and the Will. The purpose of inserting it is to give completeness to the account of the most general laws of connexion of Mind and Body, and to deal with what must ever be the most difficult problem growing out of that connexion.

Feelings and the Will, we have also some of the physiological foundations of Thought.

The First Position, named the Principle of Relativity, or
the necessity of change in order to our being conscious, is
the groundwork of Thought, Intellect, or Knowledge, as well
as of Feeling. We know heat only in the transition from
cold, and *vice versâ* ; up and down, long and short, red and
not red—are all so many transitions, or changes of impression ; and without transition we have no knowledge. Relativity applied in this way to Thought, coincides with the
power called *Discrimination*—the Sense or Feeling of
Difference, which is one of the constituents of our Intelligence. Our knowledge begins, as it were, with difference ;
we do not know any one thing of itself, but only the difference between it and another thing ; the present sensation
of heat is, in fact, a difference from the preceding cold.

The Second Position, named the Law of Diffusion,—or
the connection of Feeling with spreading currents, as
opposed to impulses that go the round in a single line,—
has bearings upon Thought likewise. Taken along with
the principle of Relativity, or Change of Impression, it
allows us, as we shall see presently, to embody the power
of Discrimination, or to assign its physical connexions with
the currents of the brain.

The Third Position had reference to the radical contrast
of Pleasure and Pain, and was meant to bring out the connection between Pleasure and a rise of Vital Power, and
between Pain and a fall of Vital Power. Although com-

plicated with the fact that stimulus, as well as nourishment, is requisite to quicken the nerve-currents to the
maximum of pleasure, this principle is a clear starting-
point for our voluntary action, otherwise without a starting-point; for the will mainly consists in following the
lead of pleasure and drawing back from the touch of
pain.

Our Intelligence, in the *practical* view, may be considered as an enormous expansion of the range of operations
under the First Law of Being—the Law of Self-Conservation. To work for the attainment of pleasure while yet
in the distance, and for the abatement of pain also in the
distance; to perform actions that are only *intermediate* in
procuring the one or avoiding the other: all this is but
voluntary action enlarged in its compass by knowledge of
cause and effect, means and end; in other words, by our
intelligent cognizance of the order of the world.

Intellect has long been divided into a variety of functions, or modes of operating, called faculties, under such
names as Memory, Reason, Judgment, Imagination, Conception, and others; which, however, are not fundamentally
distinct processes, but merely different applications of the
collective forces of the Intelligence. We have no power
of Memory in radical separation from the power of Reason
or the power of Imagination. The classification is tainted
with the fault called, in Logic, cross-division. The really
fundamental separation of the powers of the Intellect is

into three facts called (1) *Discrimination*, the Sense, Feeling, or Consciousness of Difference; (2) *Similarity*, the Sense, Feeling, or Consciousness of Agreement; and (3) *Retentiveness*, or the power of Memory or Acquisition. These three functions, however much they are mingled, and inseparably mingled, in our mental operations, are yet totally distinct properties, and each the groundwork of a different superstructure. As an ultimate analysis of the mental powers, their number cannot be increased or diminished; fewer would not explain the facts, more are unnecessary. They are the Intellect, the whole Intellect, and nothing but the Intellect.

Let us take them in order.

I. DISCRIMINATION.—This we have just seen is the intellectual aspect of Relativity, or the Law of Change of Impression. When any new currents are commenced, or when existing currents are increased or abated, we become mentally alive; and if we are already conscious, a change comes over our consciousness. It can be easily made apparent that Discrimination is the very beginning of our intellectual life. If we are insensible to the change from hot to cold we are for ever disqualified from knowing the phenomenon of heat; to be unaffected by changes of light is another way of expressing blindness; to be affected, or made conscious, by very minute shades of colour is to be highly intelligent in regard to colour. Wherever a man is more knowing than his fellows, he sees distinctions where they see none. The banker detects a bad note after it has deceived many other people.

As to the Physical Embodiment of this fact:—When we consider the vast compass of our discriminative sensibility—the seemingly innumerable shades of our consciousness in correspondence with the variety of sensible appearances, not to speak of our emotions and inner life—we begin to be aware of the need of an apparatus of great range and complication. Take any of the senses, as Sight, and consider all the degrees that we can mark between total blackness and the highest solar refulgence. Consider next the colours and their shades, and we shall find that the sensible gradations of effect are very numerous; in a mind highly endowed for colour, these felt gradations would be counted by hundreds. Again, in the Ear, a musician's discrimination of *pitch* extends, perhaps, to several hundred sounds. Our discrimination of *articulate* sounds is co-extensive with the combined alphabets of all the languages known to us.

Assuming, as we have found reason to do, that every new impression on the sense is an alteration of the currents along the track of the nerves—both the main channel and the collaterals of the diffusion—we are led to believe that consciousness is varied in two ways. First, *according to the ingress made use of,* or the particular organ and the particular nerves employed. Thus, from the eye to the ear is a perceptible transition and a new phase of consciousness. So in touch, in taste, and smell, we have a characteristic consciousness for each sense through all the varieties of sensation of that sense. We should never confound a colour with a taste. Nay more : in the higher senses, and especially in Sight and in Touch, we have differences of consciousness according to the *part* of the organ affected ; if it were not so, we should all be in the proverbial position of not knowing the right hand from the left.

In the second place, Consciousness is obviously varied according to the *energy, or other peculiarity, of the impression* made on the same organ, or part of an organ, and the same nerve. A greater impression makes a greater feeling. This of course is what we are prepared for on any hypothesis. The currents are made more intense, and a change of nervous intensity is a change of consciousness. In the senses, however, we have *qualitative* differences of sensation, which are more embarrassing to account for. To define the change of current in the optic fibres by red, yellow, and blue, and the subsequent course of diffusion, is not within our present knowledge. It has been supposed that there are separate fibres for the primitive colours, which would somewhat relieve the difficulty, and reduce the different modes of action to mere differences of intensity or degree.

These two circumstances, namely, the separate consciousness of separate nerves, and the changing intensity of the currents, we may regard as the primitive modes of diversifying the consciousness; but it is in the countless combinations of these simple elements that we are to look for the physical concomitants of our ever-varying consciousness. The union of different stimulations in different fibres and in different degrees, would unavoidably give birth to a complex and modified consciousness.

II. So much for Discrimination. Let us now glance shortly at Similarity, or AGREEMENT. Besides the shock of difference, or change, the mind is affected by the shock of agreement in the midst of difference. If a certain sensation, as redness, is felt, and if, after we have passed to something else, it recurs, there is a flash of recognition, a re-instatement of the first experience together with a feeling of recognition or identification. This is the feeling or consciousness of Agreement; it also is a great intellectual foundation. Coupled with Discrimination, it exhausts the meaning of what we call knowledge; to know anything, as a tree, is to discriminate it from all differing objects, and identify it with all agreeing objects. The extension of our knowledge of the tree is the extension of our sense of its differences and of its agreements. Similarity, in another view, is a great power of reproducing our past experience and acquisitions, an extension of the resources of Memory. By it, principally, we "ascend the brightest heaven of invention." We are perpetually reminded of objects by the presence of something of

a resembling kind. Looking at a cathedral, we readily
bring to mind other cathedrals ; hearing an anecdote,
we are almost sure to recall some one similar. Our
reason essentially consists in using an old fact in new
circumstances, through the power of discerning the agreement ; we have sown one field and seen it grow, and we
repeat the process in another field. All this is a vast
saving of the labour of acquisition ; a reduction of the
number of original growths requisite for our education.
When we have anything new to learn, as a new piece of
music, or a new proposition in Euclid, we fall back upon
our previously formed combinations, musical or geometrical,
so far as they will apply, and merely tack certain of them
together in correspondence with the new case. The
method of acquiring by patchwork sets in early, and
predominates increasingly.

III. I might go on to apply the views respecting the
corebral structure and workings, in divining the physical
process underlying this power of Similarity ; but we shall
be still better occupied in grappling with the remaining
intellectual function, RETENTIVENESS, or Memory, whose
explanation would make all the rest easy enough.

It is related by the younger Scaliger that two subjects
especially engaged the speculative curiosity of his father,
the celebrated Julius Cæsar Scaliger ; these were, the
cause of Memory and the cause of Gravity. With regard
to the last-named of the two—the nature of Gravity—we

have, since the Newtonian discovery, learned to consider
that as a solved problem, and a good example of what
constitutes finality in scientific enquiries : namely, when
we have generalized a natural connexion to the utmost,
ascertained its precise law, and traced its consequences.
That matter gravitates—that the property called Inertia
or Resistance, is united with the separate property of
attraction at all distances, we accept as a fact, and, unless
indeed we saw our way to generalizing it one step further,
we ask no more questions. So in the subject before us.
There are two very distinct natural phenomena, the one
we call consciousness or mind ; the other we call matter
and material arrangements; they are united in the most
intimate alliance. It is for us to study the nature of each
in its own way, to determine the most general laws of the
alliance, and to follow them out into the explanation of
the facts in detail ; and then, as with gravity, to rest and
be thankful.

The great scholar might, however, be forgiven for
wondering at Memory. There is nothing marvellous in
Nature's having allied this and the other mental functions
with a bodily organization ; for unless it be that the facts
called MIND and the facts called MATERIAL are the most
widely contrasted facts of our experience, and that we
have, as it were, a meeting of *extremes*, there is no more
mystery in this union than in the union of Inertia and
Gravity, Heat and Light. It is because we have something beyond the usual endowments of natural things,

in the possibility of storing up in three pounds' weight of
a fatty and albuminous tissue done into fine threads and
corpuscles, all these complicated groupings that make our
natural and acquired aptitudes and all our knowledge. If
there were sermons in stones, we should be less astonished
when they proceed from brains.

Retention, Acquisition, or Memory, then, being the
power of continuing in the mind impressions that are no
longer stimulated by the original agent, and of recalling
them at after-times by purely mental forces, I shall
remark first on the cerebral seat of those renewed
impressions. It must be considered as almost beyond a
doubt that "*the renewed feeling occupies the very same
parts, and in the same manner as the original feeling,
and no other parts, nor in any other manner that can be
assigned.*"

This view is the only one compatible with our present
knowledge of the working of the nerves, although there
formerly prevailed and still prevail other views ; the
doctrine of a common sensorium or cerebral closet where
ideas are accumulated, quite apart from the recipient
apparatus. But that view is so crude as hardly to merit
discussion. If we suppose the sound of a bell striking
the ear, and then ceasing, there is a certain continuing
impression of a feebler kind, the idea or memory of the
note of the bell ; and it would take some very good reason
to deter us from the obvious inference that the continuing

impression is the persisting (although reduced) nerve-currents aroused by the original shock. And if that be so with ideas surviving their originals, the same is likely to be the case with ideas resuscitated from the past—the remembrance of a former sound of the bell. All observation confirms the doctrine. ⸤The mental recollection of language is a suppressed articulation, ready to burst into speech⸥ When the thought of an action excites us very much, we can hardly avoid the actual repetition, so completely are all the nervous circuits repossessed with the original currents of force. The lively remembrance of a pleasant relish will produce the same expression of countenance, the very smack of the reality. Moreover, it has been determined by experiment that the persistent imagination of a bright colour fatigues the nerves of sight.*

* Great consequences follow (as it seems to me) from this view of the physical embodiment of Intellect. There grows out of it a tendency of ideas to become the full reality ; as when a person strongly imagining a kick, can scarcely refrain from the performance. The comparative weakness of the nerve-currents accompanying the idea, and the superior force of present realities, render the manifestation unfrequent in waking hours, and under ordinary conditions. Any circumstances, on the one hand, tending to intensify the idea, or, on the other hand, removing the pressure of the actual, exhibit the influence in full operation. The mesmeric sleep is the extreme instance ; the ideas suggested to the mind of the patient exclusively determine his conduct.

No fact of the human constitution more decisively proves the connexion of Intellect with the nervous system and with the moving organs and the senses. The intimacy of the alliance is shown at its utmost.

This principle is a supplementary law of the Will ; it is a stimulus to action, over and above the primary and proper motives of the Will (pleasure and pain), and often leads to conduct at variance with our interests as represented by procuring pleasure and warding off pain.

The comparative feebleness of remembered states or ideas is, we may presume, an exact counterpart of the diminished force of the revived currents of the brain. It is but seldom that the re-induced currents are equal in energy to those of direct stimulation at first hand.

And now, as to the mechanism of RETENTION.

> For every act of memory, every exercise of bodily aptitude, every habit, recollection, train of ideas, there is a specific grouping, or co-ordination, of sensations and movements, by virtue of specific growths in the cell junctions.

For example, when I see a written word and, as a result of my education, pronounce it orally, the power lies in a series of definite groupings or connexions of nerve-currents in the nerve and centres of the eye, with currents in motor nerves proceeding to the chest, larynx and mouth ; and these groupings or connexions are effected by definite growths at certain proper or convenient cell crossings.

A complication of the principle has been greatly discussed of late, under the designation of the "power of the Imagination over the body;" according to which ideas can induce healthy and morbid changes on the system. By thinking strongly on the hand, we affect the local circulation of the blood, and by persistent attention, we might set up a diseased action in the part. Applications of this peculiar affect have been suggested in medicine, and the conditions and limitations of it are deserving of careful study. It has been happily made use of by Mr. Darwin to explain Blushing.

The considerations that support us in hazarding this proposition are such as the following :—

In the first place, it is merely stating the mode of action appropriate to the structure and known workings of the brain. If the brain is a vast network of communication between sense and movement—actual and ideal—between sense and sense, movement and movement, by innumerable conducting fibres, crossing at innumerable points,—the way to make one definite set of currents induce a second definite set is in some way or other to strengthen the special points of junction where the two sets are most readily connected, so that a preference shall be established, and in that particular line of communication. The special growths accompanying memory must operate at these cell or corpuscle junctions.

Our mode of conceiving the so-called Reflex actions illustrates what I mean. A stimulus proceeds along a given nerve to a central point—a group of cells ; and there is a definite response to a certain movement, as in the closed hand of the sleeper. Now the higher connexions of mind are of the same essential character, though far surpassing in complication ; the system of freely diffused lines of communication in the brain is an obstacle to that ready selection of an outgoing channel ; and there is at first much conflict and distraction, until circumstances shall determine preference outlets, and until structural growths confirm these preferences.

The position is also fortified by the effect of diseased

points in the brain, which are known to destroy memory, often sweeping away some definite class of acquisitions or recollections, and leaving others untouched. We have now on record many remarkable cases of the destruction of the second and third frontal convolutions of the brain accompanied by loss of speech, while the intellectual faculties generally were unimpaired.

In the next place, Acquisition has a limit, determined by the amount of the nervous substance, that is, the size of the brain.

We are apt to be carried away with a vague notion that there is no limit to acquirement, except our defect of application or some other curable weakness of our own. There are, however, very manifest limits. We are all blockheads in something; some of us fail in mechanical aptitude, some in music, some in languages, some in science. Memory, in one of these lines of incapacity, is a rope of sand; there must be in each case a deficiency of cerebral substance for that class of connexions.

Then, again, there is a tendency in acquisitions to decay unless renewed. Hence, a time must come in the progress of acquisition when the whole available force of growth is needed in order to conserve what we have already got; when, in fact, we are losing at one end as much as we gain at the other.

It is further to be remarked that much of our mental improvement in later life is the *substitution* of a better class of judgments for our first immature notions, these

last being gradually dropped. There is not necessarily
more room occupied in the brain by a good opinion than
by a bad, when once the good opinion is arrived at ; or by
an elegant gesture as compared with an awkward one.

Even taking the regular student, whose life is spent in
amassing knowledge, we find that his memory at last, if it
does not refuse the new burdens, gives them place by
letting go much that has been previously learned. Moreover, a wide scholarship turns into a knowledge of the
places where knowledge is. It is only a limited range
of ideas that any one can command at any one time ;
although in the course of a life we may shift into several
successive spheres of intellectual range.

Farther, we have seen, in alluding to the power of
Similarity or Agreement, that one acquisition is made to
serve on many different occasions. A new word is a group
of old articulations ; a new air to a musician, a new
manipulation to a chemist, is merely a slight variation
of some previous acquirement.

Once more. In a vast number of instances, what we
retain is not so much certain ready-made combinations, as
the means for putting these together when required. This
is well exemplified in the economy of names. By
means of combining generic and specific names, two
or three thousand words can suffice to name one hundred
thousand plants. So in ordinary language: the suffix
"ness," understood once for all, enables us to convert
thirteen hundred adjectives into abstract nouns; so that

the recollection of these abstract nouns involves no independent effort. And, in like manner, instead of having
in the memory trains of formed sentences for every
occasion, we have a certain number of forms that can be
freely accommodated to the matter we wish to express.

And finally, the great principle of the Will is, by its
nature, self-correcting, after trial and error. This comes
in place of many nice adjustments, and renders a sentient
framework superior to all other machines. It is not
necessary to the power of imitation that a sound heard
should at once suggest the exact vocal articulation for
reproducing the effect: something may be at first
suggested not quite up to the sound: the sense of dis-
crepancy then checks it; other movements arise and are
likewise checked; and so on till the coincidence is reached.

I will now venture upon a hypothetical comparison
between these two things—our Acquisitions on the one
hand, and the number of the Nervous elements of the
brain on the other.

A certain number of definite groupings or co-ordinations
must be allowed to our various Instincts; as, for example,
the combined movements of the heart, intestines, and
lungs, and the special modifications of them in swallowing,
coughing, and sucking. The simplicity and the limitation
of these acts are such as to require comparatively few
pre-established groupings. When to the simple instincts
of Organic Life we add the *higher instincts* included in our

Feelings, and their embodiment in our Voluntary powers, and even in our Intelligence, the number is enlarged on a scale corresponding with the acquired aptitudes; and the new theory is that these higher instincts are all hereditary, or transmitted acquisitions.

Our Acquisitions taken as a whole represent the great mass of our nervous growths. I shall attempt to give a rough classification of them :—

1. The simpler and earlier Voluntary Aptitudes, implied in the voluntary control of the various moving members, as the hand. We have not originally the power of moving any part in a definite way to execute a purpose; we have to associate the several movements with the effects to be produced. With the sight of a morsel of food, and the state of hunger, we associate the definite movement of the hand to the mouth. With the feeling of morsel in the mouth, we have to associate definite movements of the tongue and the jaw. These are groupings of a considerable degree of complication. A visible image, with the knowledge of what the vision suggests, as, for example, a bit of sugar, and a feeling or craving based on a recollection of the past,—concur as a definite situation; and that situation has to be followed by a grasping movement of the hand, and a subsequent movement towards the mouth; to which succeeds a series of movements in the mouth itself. The exercise of the voluntary powers is a manifold repetition of the same fact—a

definite situation followed by a definite group or series
of movements.

2. The Muscular Groupings in the various experiences
of Resistance, Size, Form, and allied properties. These
are embodied in the hand, the arm, and the locomotive
organs generally, and in the allied nervous centres for
motor currents. Without the special senses, as Sight
these notions are very vague, showing that the provision
for the nervous embodiment of movements is not great.
Still we can discriminate degrees of force, by the muscles
alone ; to every distinguishable degree there must be a
definite and distinct nervous track ; and to every association with each special degree, there must correspond an
appropriate nervous grouping, disentangled from all other
groupings. With every distinguishable weight we form
some separate associations, some actions to be performed
when that weight is felt, as in sorting, according to weight,
heavy and light things.

The groupings in the muscles of the Eye that correspond to visible motions and forms, are exceedingly
numerous. These enter into our highest intellectual
acquirements of visible pictures and arrangements. A
circle is a series of ocular movements, in definite march and
grouping ; for this one effect hundreds of currents are
excited in individual fibres and cells.

The groupings of the Larynx, Tongue, and Mouth, for
vocal exertions, and above all for articulate speech, are

H

on a vast scale.   As with every simple form visible
to the eye, so with every separate articulate sound—
every letter in the alphabet—there is a complex series
of situations, graduated and organized in the corresponding centres, whether pure motor, or motor and
sensory combined.

3. Although there is a propriety in viewing the muscular
associations as a distinct branch of our mental framework, they are, in point of fact, always blended with the
special senses; and the delicacy of discrimination is far
higher in the pure and proper senses than in the muscles
alone.   By the pure senses are meant, Touch (without
strain or pressure), Taste, Smell, Hearing, Sight (in its
optical part).   To every discriminated sensation there is
(we must believe) a distinct and characteristic group of
currents, actuating a separate group of fibres and cells,
and susceptible of being united with any definite movement or any other definite sensation.   Now even in
the inferior senses, the grades of discrimination are
numerous; in Taste and Smell, probably hundreds; in
Hearing and Sight, thousands.   In the quality of musical
Pitch, a fine ear can discriminate a small fraction of a
tone; in a range of seven octaves a great many separate
sensations could be held apart without being confounded.
If to pitch we add Intensity, Volume, and Timbre, the
discriminations would be multiplied in proportion.   Still,
however, the discriminations held in the memory are

not so numerous as we might suppose from the delicacy of comparing the *actual* sensations.

The Eye, by its optical function, takes in grades of Light and Shade, mixtures of white and dark in the series of Greys, and varieties of Colour. A good eye might have several hundreds of distinct optical gradations in these various effects. But the eye shows its great compass in the plurality of combinations of points or surfaces of different light, making up what are commonly called *images:* compounds of visible form (muscular) and visible groupings (optical). The multitude of these that can be distinctly embodied and remembered would seem to defy computation; yet every one must have its own track in that labyrinth of fibres and corpuscles called the brain.

4. Thus, in the muscular feelings, and in the sensations of the special senses, there are all these various grades of distinguishable states of feeling, and an enormous number of connexions between them in our memory of things and of events. Yet farther. Movements may be associated with sensations in every one of the senses; and there may be associations between each sense and all the others:—Touches, with tastes, smells, sounds, sights; Tastes, with smells, sounds, and sights; Smells, with sounds and sights; and, most of all, Sounds with sights. What we call our knowledge of a thing is the union of all the sensations produced by it into a complex

idea of that thing. The idea of a shilling is a compound of visible appearance, sound, and touch.

5. All these simpler combinations are themselves re-compounded into still higher combinations. The far-reaching and all-embracing acquisition, called Language, is based on the articulate groupings; these are formed into words, words into phrases and sentences; and all tho while there is a process of adhesion between each verbal element and some object of sight or other sense. The vocal articulation in uttering the word "sun," the sound it makes on the ear when pronounced, the appearance of the thing,—are all united in one higher grouping or complex intellectual product. Words are thus joined to things; trains of words are joined to trains of events. In learning foreign languages, words as sounds are joined to other words as sounds, visible symbols to visible symbols; trains of words in both capacities to other trains. As we can readily compute the number of words making up the vocabulary of a language, we have a means of setting forth in a sort of numerical estimate the extent of our acquisitions, and the number of independent brain-growths that correspond to these.

Every *special acquirement* is a re-compounding of the elementary groupings above sketched. A science, for example, such as Arithmetic, is a vast aggregate of new sensible groupings; the elements being our notions of number gained from numbered things, the ten ciphers, and their union in the decimal system. There is here a great process of economy. The multiplication table, which contains 144 propositions, or statements of the equivalence of numbers, is a weapon of indefinite power in computation. Still a great deal of independent acquisition must succeed these embodiments of the multiplication table; many farther rules must be learnt, with exemplifying instances. To work vulgar and decimal fractions demands the forming of new and complicated ties. Conceive, then, the amount of distinctive nervous embodiment in one arithmetical fact, as "six times ten is sixty :" one hundred and forty-four such are needed for the table; while the table itself is really a very small portion of the growths in the mind of a fair arithmetician, even allowing for the process, so abundantly exemplified in science, of making the old serve in the new. Supposing the table were one-fiftieth of the memorial embodiment of any one's Arithmetical powers; the nervous growths would be upwards of seven thousand for this one subject. Five more sciences of like compass would give more than forty thousand groupings; but there would be a very great condensation through unavoidable repetitions. Still an accomplished mathematician might have upwards of twenty or thirty thousand groupings of the degree of complicacy typified in the table; there being, however, a considerable number of trains equal in length to several columns of the table.

In learning an air of music, suppose the Old Hundredth Psalm Tune, there is a definite succession of notes. We may view the embodiment of such an acquisition in this way. The first note suggests nothing; three or four are needed to determine the air. With the sequence of, say, four notes, is associated the fifth, and at the same time the name and all other adjuncts of the air. A complex situation is thereby created, and with that the succeeding notes are all associated in train. About thirty notes are thus enchained in a fixed order; each note being the associated sequel of a group of notes, or other mental effects, of at least three or four members. There are thus nearly thirty associations of some complicacy in this single air. A good musician has hundreds of such sequences; perhaps upwards of a thousand, but not less than a thousand. Great allowance must be made for repetitions. A musical education would thus comprise as many as twenty thousand separate associations of small determining groups of notes with other notes.

It is on this analogy that we should have to express the verbal memory for consecutive statements. The determining words of a passage—two, three, or four in number,—will commence the train; every new word is associated with a prior group of words and meanings.

6. In the acquired connexions with the Feelings or Emotions, and in those associations of Will called the "Moral Habits," we might exemplify a distinct and somewhat peculiar class of growths. The number is still very great; as is apparent when we reflect upon the great multitude of things connected in our mind with pleasurable and painful feelings. The peculiarity lies in the greater impetus or power in every wave that involves either feeling or an exercise of will. To this impetus must correspond a burst of nervous power, and for that burst we seem to need a certain mass of nervous substance—a large body of corpuscles roused into activity. Think of the strain necessary to maintain a struggle of the will against a strong present appetite. In such a case as this, the corpuscles of the brain must act not solely as junctions for establishing complicated groupings, but as sources of energy; and they need to be multiplied in that view. Size of brain, or multitude of nerve-elements—fibres and corpuscles—does not follow Intellect alone, but varies with the need of motive muscular power; to which we must now add energy of emotional manifestations and of will or volitional impulses. Accordingly, a considerable share of the nervous elements has to be assigned to the class of growths now mentioned.

There is a nice question raised, as to whether the three functions—Intellect, Emotion or Feeling, and Will, are separately located in the brain. The likelihood is that Intellectual combinations and Feelings go together; with this difference, that the currents of Feelings or Emotions have a wider diffusion and more forcible impetus, and find their way to the motor centres at large, evoking what is called the Expression of-feeling. The primitive shocks of Feeling, are at once intellectual and emotional, but may afterwards be developed more in the one direction than in the other; yet every intellectual exertion has an emotional side, every emotional outburst an intellectual side.

The association of objects with Feelings is an immense power in the Mind; it governs very largely the pleasurable and painful susceptibilities of mature life. According to the doctrine of Evolution, this class of growths becomes hereditary, and accounts for our special emotions, as Fear, Love, and Anger.

Let us put together these and other indications of the extent of the human acquisitions demanding separate and independent nervous embodiments. Take the case of learning languages, where the numerical estimate is approximately attainable. We can count the number of words in a language; we can make allowance for the repetition of the same root-word in different compounds. The association of a word with a simple meaning, as sun, fire, hill, food, presents a limited, though still considerable, degree of complication. The association of one name with another in a foreign tongue, is a still simpler conjunction.

I may cite as an illustration the Chinese language, with its forty thousand characters. The strongest memory is incapable of retaining these : indeed a very unusual stretch of memory is requisite to keep hold of the ten thousand needed for the ordinary literature.   Again, consider the situation of a Philologist knowing six cultivated languages and ten uncultivated vocabularies (of several hundred vocables each).   Such an acquirement would use up little less than half the attention and plasticity of one's life.   If, then, this education were represented by fifty thousand cerebral connexions, of variable complication, but many of them very simple, as word to word, we could assign a rough valuation to the magnitude of our possible acquisitions.

The rival department to language, as regards variety and amount, is the department of visual recollections, or pictorial groupings and spectacle.   Here, too, we reach a limit.   A datum for calculation might be, how many faces could we remember, and associate with names and other accompaniments ?   Not certainly more than two or three thousand.   So with the remembrance of localities, as the streets of towns.   A life would not suffice for laying up in the memory the streets of London.

Such an object as the human face and figure might seem an enormous complication.   Every feature has its form, size, and colouring; and the comprehension of such an aggregate would appear to demand an immense aggregate of sense impressions, and use up a very large area of nervous connexions.   This complication, however, is delusive.   The memory does not retain a coloured photograph, but only a few salient and deciding marks; perhaps not more than from six to ten indications of form, size, and colour. These are enough for identification, and we do not retain any more, except in cases of very peculiar intimacy.

A Naturalist, with all the aids of classification, cannot retain in his memory the marks of more than perhaps two or three thousand species; for the rest he must be content to refer to his books. Yet he, too, must have devoted the larger half of the plastic energy of his brain to his special studies.

The conclusion is that the cerebral growths, of a certain typical complication, cannot be adequately stated in hundreds; they amount to thousands, and even tens of thousands; they scarcely count by hundreds of thousands.

Let us make a rough estimate of the nervous elements —fibres and corpuscles—with a view to compare the number of these with the number of our acquisitions.

The thin cake of grey substance, surrounding the hemispheres of the brain, and extended into many doublings by the furrowed or convoluted structure, is somewhat difficult to measure. It has been estimated at upwards of 300 square inches, or as nearly equal to a square surface of 18 inches in the side. Its thickness is variable, but, on an average, it may be stated at one-tenth of an inch. It is the largest accumulation of grey matter in the body. It is made up of several layers of grey substance divided by layers of white substance. The grey substance is a nearly compact mass of corpuscles, of variable size. The large caudate nerve-cells are mingled with very small corpuscles, less than the thousandth of an inch in diameter. Allowing for intervals, we may suppose that a linear row of five hundred cells occupies an inch; thus giving a quarter of a million to the square inch, for 300 inches. If one half of the thickness of the layer is made up of fibres, the corpuscles or cells, taken by themselves, would be a mass one twentieth of an inch thick, say sixteen cells in the depth. Multiplying these numbers together, we should reach a total of twelve hundred millions of cells in the grey covering of the hemispheres. As every cell is united with at least two fibres, often many more, we may multiply this number by four, for the number of connecting fibres attached to the mass; which gives four thousand eight hundred millions of fibres. Assume the respective numbers to be (corpuscles) one thousand, and (fibres) five thousand, millions, and make the comparison with our acquisitions as follows :—

With a total of 50,000 Acquisitions, evenly spread over the whole of the hemispheres, there would be for each nervous grouping at the rate of 20,000 cells and 100,000 fibres.

With a total of 200,000 Acquisitions of the assumed types, which would certainly include the most retentive and most richly-endowed minds, there would be for each nervous grouping 5000 cells and 25,000 fibres.

This leaves out of account a very considerable mass of nervous matter in the spinal cord, medulla oblongata, cerebellum, and the lesser grey centres of the brain; in all of which there are very large deposits of grey matter, with communicating white fibres to match.

Such an estimate, confined to the hemispheres of the brain, is enough for its purpose, which is to show that numerous as are the embodiments to be provided for, the nervous elements are on a corresponding scale, and that there is no improbability in supposing an independent nervous track for each separate acquisition.

It is not at all likely, however, that the entire brain can be partitioned equally among the various subjects to be remembered or acquired. Besides the fact that a great part of the brain substance exists for mere battery power—to propel muscles, and to keep up energetic volitions and manifestations of feeling—there seems often to be a duplication of the same embodiment in different parts. The two hemispheres apparently repeat one another; when one is injured, the other keeps up the trains of memory, although with weakened energies. It is even supposed that in the same hemisphere there may be duplicates; since injuries in the forepart of the head have occurred without destroying any single class of acquisitions. Moreover, it is most unlikely that a perfect economy of the cells and fibres can be realized, however well distributed the acquisitions may be. Could we bring all the elements into full play, there might possibly be room for many times our present average store of recollections.

We may go one step further, and enquire how the various groupings may arise, and how they can be isolated so as to preserve the requisite distinctness in our trains of thought. Let me first call attention to the difficulties of the case.

If each set of sensory fibres had one definite connexion with motory or outcarrying fibres, we should have always the same movement answering to the stimulation of the same nerves, as in the reflex system; the fibre a could do nothing but effect the movement x. It is necessary to the variety and flexibility of our acquirements, that the fibre a should at one time take part in stimulating x, and at another time take part in stimulating y, the circumstances being different. The stroke of the clock will stimulate us at one time to set out in one direction, and at another time in another direction, according to the ideas that *it co-operates with.* Then, again, the *degree* of the stimulation of the same fibres will determine, not merely a greater energy of the same response, as would happen in reflex stimulation, but a totally different response: a, *weak*, determines movement x; a, *strong*, determines y. The steersman of a ship making for port is guided by the intensity of the beacon light.

These illustrations show the two chief conditions where-

by the same nerve is instrumental in causing distinct
movements, namely—

　　1st. Its being differently grouped.

　　2nd. Its being unequally stimulated.

We shall begin with the case of *difference of grouping.*
The fibre *a* stimulated along with *b* gives *x;* so *a c*
gives *y,* and *b c* gives *z.*

Let us try and imagine how the structure is adapted to
this state of things. It requires us to assume, not merely
fibres multiplying by ramification through the cell junctions, but also an extensive arrangement of *cross connec-
tions.* We can typify it in this way. Suppose *a* enters a
cell junction, and is replaced by several branches, *a', a',*
&c. ; *b,* in like manner, is multiplied into *b', b',* &c. Let
one of the branches of *a,* or *a',* pass into some second cell,
and a branch of *b,* or *b',* pass into the same, and let one of
the emerging branches be *X,* we have then a means for
connecting united *a* and *b* with *X ;* and, in some other
crossing, a branch of *a* may unite with a branch of *c,* from
which crossing *Y* emerges, and so on. In every case
of united stimulation producing a definite movement, we
must suppose a set of cells where ramifications of the
stimulated nerves unite themselves, and find an outlet of
communication with that special movement.

The diagram shows the arrangement. The fibre *a*
branches into two *a', a' ;* the fibre *b,* into *b', b' ; c* into
c', c'. One of the branches of *a* unites with one of the

branches of b, or a' b' in a cell X; b' c' unite in Y; a' c' in Z. These cells X, Y, Z, are supposed to be the commencement of motor fibres, each communicating with a separate muscular group, and rousing a distinctive movement. By this plan we comply with the primary condition of assigning a separate outcome to every different combination of sensory impressions.

Fig. 2.

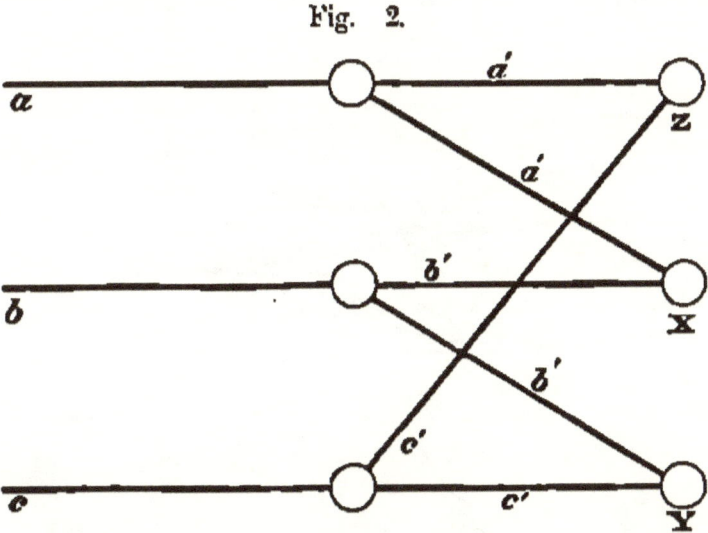

We may compare this diagram with the following, given by Dr. Lionel Beale, to show the manner of junction of nerve fibres with caudate nerve cells. The crossing of fibres from one cell to collateral cells is exactly what is supposed in the foregoing representation. Dr. Beale is not advocating any theory of the physical basis of our in-

tellectual acquisitions; his object is to represent the connexions of fibres and corpuscles as actually exhibited. The
conformity of his diagram with the scheme of cross con-
nections required by the foregoing hypothetical scheme, is
very striking. But, indeed, without a most extensive
system of these lateral communications, we should be
wholly unable to imagine the embodiment of our distinctive mental impressions.

Fig. 3.

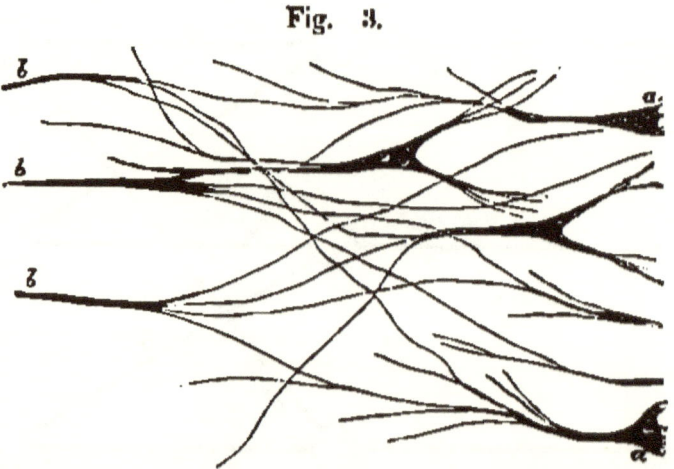

We have taken the simplest case possible—binary
groupings of three elements, *a*, *b*, *c*. The diagram
shews that for these we need three primary fibres,
six branching fibres, and six cells. Our acquisitions
involve far more complex groupings. To give a distinctive
character to the most ordinary impression on the eye, or

the ear, there is commonly a union of four, five, six, seven, or more, separate impressions, as in the letters of a word, the characters of a piece of furniture, the marks of an individual person; and each of these elementary or constituent impressions—a letter of the alphabet, a round or square form,—is already a complex compound. Hence the number of fibres and cells brought into action, before the grouping can converge upon some one set of cells definitely connected with an out-going motor arrange-ment, or with some other internal grouping,—must be very great indeed; and but for the vast number of fibres and cells, demonstrably present in the brain, the separate embodiment of every separate impression and idea would seem impracticable.

Next as to *unequal intensities* of stimulation of the same nerves:—*a*, weak, is connected with X; *a*, stronger, with Y; *a*, still stronger, with Z. When you taste a cup of tea, you give utterance to the word "weak" under one pitch of sensation; at another pitch, the same nerves being affected, you give forth the word "good." On a fine ear, the same fibres may discriminate many shades of in-tensity, and may for every one be associated differently with vocal exertions. Now, a more energetic current necessarily takes *a more extended sweep*, and affects a number of cells and fibres that are left quiescent under a feebler current. The cells being viewed as *crossings* —where a current in one circuit induces a current in an

I

adjoining circuit—there is, at each crossing, a certain resistance to overcome, and the feebler current is sooner exhausted and stops short of the distance reached by stronger. It is like a larger wave on the sea-shore, whose superior bulk and impetus are made most conspicuous by outstripping all the rest as it rushes up the sands. We may figure the action thus:—

A certain intensity makes an effective induction (in the electrical sense of the word "induction"), suppose once; the currents so generated do not produce a second induction of the same power. A weak current in a certain line of fibres produces, we shall say, a hundred *secondary* currents, which amount of diffusion gives to it its character in the consciousness, and its local habitation where it meets outgoing motor currents. But a stronger impetus will determine all these hundred secondary currents, and a hundred *tertiary* besides, which will make the character of its diffusion; and the points where a number of the secondary concur with a number of the tertiary will be the points where a definite motor current may be associated with it. So that what begins as mere difference of intensity in one track ends in difference of grouping, or in characteristic points of meeting, whence a definite motor current may take its rise, and be distinctively united.

The following diagram gives the supposed arrangement. The fibre *a* enters a cell, and three others emerge, marked *a'*. Each of these enters other cells, and there emerge a new set of fibres, marked *a'*. One of the first branchings,

a^1, is seen at the top of the figure proceeding with a second branching, a^2, to the cell marked X.   This con-

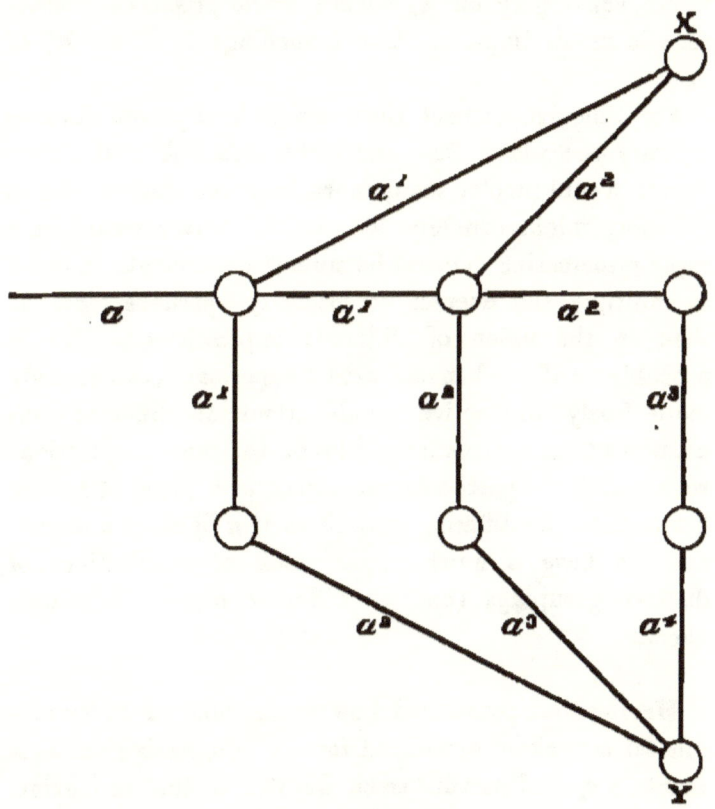

a¹ and a³ give X
a², a³, and a⁴ give Y.

vergence would represent the lowest degree of intensity. A higher degree of intensity makes a larger sweep,

affecting both second, third, and fourth branchings ; a
grouping made up of these is seen at the bottom of the
figure, converging on Y, whence would proceed a characteristic motor impulse. The branchings to Y are a', a^2
and a'.

For this arrangement there are at least eleven fibres—
primary, secondary, &c.—and eight cells. A next higher
degree would involve many more, in order that a definite
grouping might converge at a point. There would be a
rapidly increasing demand for numerous elements, in order
to multiply the degrees of intensity—perhaps more so
than in the union of different impressions.   This is
probably confirmed in our actual experience ; we embody
more freely distinctive combinations of different impressions than various intensities of the same impression :
we remember a parti-coloured object, as a piece of tartan,
better than the differing intensities of a light, or a sound :
and we have a much larger stock of recollections of
distinct groupings than of different degrees of single
effects.

Having thus considered how to provide, for every new
mental connexion demanded for our progressive acquirements, a special nervous track devoted to that connexion,
the remaining point is to consider by what means the
connexions are permanently fixed in the several tracks.
This is to assign the physical bond underlying memory,
recollection, or the retentive power of the mind.

We know what are the conditions of making an acquirement, or of fixing two or more things together in the memory.   The separate impressions must be made together, or flow in close succession; and they must be held together for a certain length of time, either on one occasion, or on repeated occasions.   Now to each impression, each sensation or thought, there corresponds physically a group or series of nerve-currents; when two impressions concur, or closely succeed one another, the nerve-currents find some bridge or place of continuity, better or worse, according to the abundance of nerve-matter available for the transition.   In the cells or corpuscles where the currents meet and join, there is, in consequence of the meeting, a *strengthened connexion* or *diminished obstruction*—a preference track for that line over other lines where no continuity has been established.

This is merely a hypothetical rendering of the facts: yet it is a very probable rendering.   In the nature and number of the nerve elements, and their mode of connexion, there is nothing hypothetical; and there is no departure from fact or strong probability, in assigning special and distinct tracks for the currents connected with each separate sensation, idea, emotion, or other conscious state.   As to the precise mode of the plastic growth that unites separate impressions into trains and aggregates in the memory,—we know that the corpuscles or crossings are the points that must be operated upon; that a flow of healthy blood must co-operate to the effect; and that the

process takes time. It is evidently a species of growth :
but the precise molecular change effected in the lines of
strengthened communication, or diminished obstruction,
we can describe only as increasing the conducting tendency
in those lines, as compared with the collateral openings
where no such operation has taken place.*

* In thus endeavouring to sketch the embodiment of our intellectual
functions in the cerebral system, I have been very much aided by the
views and the diagrams of Dr. Lionel Beale. Almost every one of the
views peculiar to him assist the foregoing speculation.

1. As regards the connexion of the nerve-cells, Dr. Beale maintains
that all true nerve-cells are continuous with nerve-fibres, and have at
least two such connexions. The so-called *apolar* cells—having no
visible communication with fibres—are without meaning on any
hypothesis of nervous action hitherto suggested. Moreover, while it is
admitted that there may be as few as two nerve connexions, a large
proportion of cells must have more than two, otherwise nerve-fibres
would have to rise in the brain as loose ends.

2. With respect to the minuteness, and consequently the number, of
the ultimate nerve fibres, Dr. Beale supposes that the so-called ultimate
fibre (the dark-bordered fibre, varying from 1-3000th to 1-15000th of an
inch) may be in reality a bundle, and that the true ultimate fibres are
represented by the terminal ramifying fibres of 1-100,000th of an inch, or
less. Now upon the supposition of a distinct nervous track, or series of
connexions, for each distinct acquirement, the number of the fibres
must correspond to the number of acquirements ; and the greater
the number actually proved to exist, the more credible is the hypothesis
of separate embodiment.

3. The manner of connexion of the nerve-fibres with the cell, and
with one another through the cell, is conjectured and figured by Dr.
Beale in a plan that facilitates our conception of the physical growths
underlying memory and acquisition. (I refer particularly to his paper
in the Proceedings of the Royal Society, vol. xili., p. 386, on the Paths of
Nerve-currents in Nerve-cells.) He observed, in certain specimens of
the caudate nerve-cells, a series of lines passing across the body of the
cell, and continuing into its branches, or communicating with the
nerves. He considers these lines as the tracks of nervous action through
the cell, being probably somewhat different in substance from the rest

of the matter of the cell.   He couples with this appearance the doctrine
(maintained by him, although disputed by others) that the nerves
terminate in loops, and consequently form an unbroken nervous
circuit.   He then suggests that the cell-crossing is the place where the
inner bendings of a great many independent circuits come into close
neighbourhood, and affect one another by a process of the nature of
electrical induction.   Any one of the circuits being active, or excited,
would impart excitement to all that came near it in the same cell.   (See
fig. 3 of the paper referred to.)

Now assuming such an arrangement, I can suppose that, at first, each
one of the circuits would affect all the others indiscriminately; but
that, in consequence of two of them being independently made active at
the same moment (which is the fact in acquisition), a strengthened
connexion or diminished obstruction would arise between these two, by
a change wrought in the intervening cell-substance; and that, afterwards, the induction from one of these circuits would not be indis-
criminate, but select; being comparatively strong towards one, and
weaker towards the rest.

CHAPTER VI.

HOW ARE MIND AND BODY UNITED?

A VAST deal of speculation has been expended as to the manner of union of Mind and Body. The majority of persons are disposed to treat the question as insoluble, as unsuited to our faculties, as what is termed a "mystery."

This word "mystery" is itself greatly misconceived. Such was the opinion of one of the ablest of biblical critics—Principal George Campbell—as to the employment of the word in religious doctrine. In Campbell's view "μυστήριον" means simply what we call a secret—a thing for the time concealed, but afterwards to be made known. It is the correlative term to "Revelation," which disclosed what had previously been hidden.

In another acceptation, Mystery is correlated to Explanation; it means something intelligible enough as a fact, but not accounted for, not reduced to any law, principle, or reason. The ebb and flow of the Tides, the motion of the Planets, Satellites, and Comets, were understood as facts at all times; but they were regarded as mysteries until Newton brought them under the Laws of Motion and of Gravity. Earthquakes and volcanoes are still mysterious; their explanation is not yet fully made out. The immediate derivation of muscular power and of animal heat is unknown, which renders these phenomena mysterious.

The meaning of the correlative couple—Mystery, Explanation—has been rendered precise by the march of physical science since the age of Newton. Mystery is the isolation of a fact from all others. Explanation is the discerning of agreement among facts remotely placed: it is essentially the *generalizing process*, whereby many widely scattered appearances are shown to come under one commanding principle or law. The fall of a stone, the flow of rivers, the retention of the moon in her circuit, are all expressed by the single law of Gravity. This generalizing sweep is a real advance in our knowledge, an ascent in the scale of intelligence, a step towards the centralization of the empire of science; and it is the only real meaning of Explanation. A difficulty is solved, a mystery is unriddled, according as the mysterious fact can be shown to resemble other facts. Mystery is solitariness, exception, or it may be apparent contradiction; the resolution of the mystery is found in assimilation, identity, fraternity. When all natural operations are assimilated, as far as assimilation can go, as far as likeness holds, there is an end to explanation, and to the necessity for it; there is an end to what the mind can intelligently desire; perfect vision is consummated.

But, say many persons, after resolving the fall of a stone and the sun's attraction into one force called

gravity, there still remains the mystery—what is gravity?
Even Newton sought to explain gravity itself. Well, if
you must go farther, find some other force to *assimilate*
with gravity; you will then make a new generalizing
stride, and achieve a farther step of explanation. If, however, there is no other force to be assimilated, gravity is
the final term of explanation, the full revelation of the
mystery. There is nothing farther to be done; nothing
farther to be desired. Nor have we here any reason to be
dissatisfied with this position, to complain of baulked
satisfaction, or of being on a lower platform than we
might possibly occupy. Our intelligence is fully honoured,
fully implemented, by the possession of a principle as wide
in its sweep as the phenomenon itself.

Apply all this to the union of Mind and Body. These
two phenomena have very little in common; they parti-
cipate only in the most general attributes, namely,
Quantity, Co-existence, and Succession, and even as
regards these their participation is limited.

As to *Quantity*, Degree, or distinction of More and
Less, there is no exemption on the part of either. The
properties of every material body are distinguished as
more or less; magnitude, weight, colour, hardness, &c.,
have assignable degrees or amounts specific to each
substance. So also are the mental properties distinguished
as more or less; our pleasures, our pains, our thoughts,
may be numbered and measured, although the grades of

intensity of the feelings cannot be assigned with the same minute precision that belongs to the leading material properties, such as size, weight, or tenacity. Again, material properties *co-exist;* a plurality may concur in the same object ; a diamond has size, form, transparency, and other qualities, all co-inhering in the same unity. So mental attributes co-inhere, are attached to a common subject ; the same mind feels, wills, and thinks. Lastly, Material phenomena are in a state of change or mutation ; they show successive phases ; and in their *succession* we recognise the peculiar and remarkable bond termed Causation, or Cause and Effect. A spark falls into water, it is extinguished ; it falls on gunpowder, there is an explosion. The same fluctuation, mutation, succession, and causation, may be traced in the workings of mind ; a pain suddenly ceasing, is followed by a re-action of pleasure.

The one feature usually signalized as present in all material phenomena, and absent from all states of the conscious mind, is that mode of Co-existence called Order in Place, EXTENSION. A building or a tree is named as an extended thing ; a pleasure, a pain, a recollection, is not felt to be extended ; there is an incompatibility between a feeling and a perception of extended magnitude. While we are mentally occupied or engrossed with a genial warmth, we are not able to entertain the perception of a room, or a fire, as occupying space.

Bodily facts and mental facts are in themselves equally

conceivable, equally intelligible.   When we see a table we
perceive it in the way suited to our faculties ; there is no
reservation or mystery attached to it as a table.   When
we feel a warm surface, we have a sufficient notion of
what warmth is.   There is a marked difference of nature
between these two feelings ; they differ much more than
a table differs from a house, or the taste of sugar from
the sound of an Æolian harp.   Yet difference does not
interfere with knowledge, but on the contrary adds to it ;
every new difference is the revelation of a new quality.

I repeat, what a piece of matter is, what an operation of
mind is, we know equally well ; we see that they both
agree and differ from other kinds of matter, and from
other operations of mind.   There is a much closer kindred
between material facts among themselves, and between
mental facts among themselves, than between material
facts generally and mental facts generally.   Hence, we
resolve all the facts of nature ultimately into two kinds—
matter and mind ; and we do not resolve these into
anything higher.   We come upon a wider contrast at this
point than we had in any prior stage of our generalizing
movement.   The Plants and the Animals differ widely in
their details ; both differ still more widely from Inanimate
Matter.   Yet they agree in all the principal features of
material bodies ; and are in total opposition to mind,
which has neither the distinctive features of either, nor
the common attributes of both.   The inanimate and the
animate are not so different as body and mind.

Extension is but the first of a long series of properties all present in matter, all absent in mind. INERTIA cannot belong to a pleasure, a pain, an idea, as experienced in the consciousness; it can belong only to the physical accompaniments of mind—the overt acts of volition, and the manifestations of feeling. Inertia is accompanied with GRAVITY, a peculiarly material property. So COLOUR is a truly material property, it cannot attach to a feeling, properly so called, a pleasure or a pain. These three properties are the basis of matter; to them are superadded, FORM, MOTION, POSITION, and a host of other properties expressed in terms of these—Attractions and Repulsions, Hardness, Elasticity, Cohesion, Crystallization, Heat, Light, Electricity, Chemical properties, Organized properties (in special kinds of matter).

When we have laid out in full array the properties peculiar to matter, and the properties peculiar to mind, we present two distinct departments of study, having each its difficulties to be overcome. Matter in many of its properties is simple, intelligible, devoid of all mystery, the very type of plainness; such are Extension, Inertia, Gravity. It has other properties less known, but yet not altogether unintelligible, as Heat, Light, Electricity, Chemical attraction. A third class are still less understood, and verge on the mysterious, as the Vital properties. We do not fully understand how the nutritive processes yield muscular motion; we cannot assimilate the fact with any other known facts, or bring it under any known law.

Mind, in some of its phenomena, is plain enough. We distinguish Pleasures and Pains, we know many of the laws of their rise, subsidence, and mutual action. We know as a fact that our thoughts follow in trains, and we can resolve many of the successions into general laws of succession; which is, up to a certain point, to explain the phenomena. We are less acquainted with the laws governing the successions in dreaming; these successions are by comparison mysterious to us.

There are thus two knowledges, each advancing on its own way, and gradually extending the region of the plain and intelligible at the expense of the obscure, the isolated, and the unintelligible. So far, there is nothing that any one can complain of, excepting the slowness of our progress. But now we have to take account of a new fact, namely, that these two classes of properties are conjoined in the unity of a sentient being—man or animal. The same being that exhibits the mental powers, is a lump of matter, characterized by a great number of the most subtle endowments of matter. A sentient animal has two endowments, two sides or aspects of its being—the one all matter, the other all mind. Notwithstanding the cardinal opposition of the two sets of powers, they are inseparably joined in the same being; they co-inhere in the one individual, man or animal. This may seem curious or wonderful, but there is nothing in it to take umbrage at. If mind exists, it must exist somewhere and somehow; for anything we know, it might have existed

apart, in a way that we cannot figure to ourselves for
want of some example within our reach. In actual fact,
it exists in company with a peculiar mass of matter,
containing in a very superior degree the properties known
as living or organized. Mind is not associated with
mineral or inanimate matter. Does this conjunction interfere with our study of the two separate departments—
mind and body—each according to its kind ? Apparently
not. It cannot interfere with our observation of all those
material properties in minerals and vegetables that exist
without an alliance with mental powers. It need not interfere with the study even of the highly organized functions
of animals, unless these are somehow or other controlled
by mental operations, which can be known only by actual
examination.

We might thus, to all appearance, proceed in our separate tracts of material and of mental investigation, in spite
of the incorporation of the mental with the material in
certain living subjects. But now, are we to take any
notice of the fact of the *union itself ?* Are we to enun-
ciate as a property of matter, that a certain highly complicated material mass can be associated with mind ; and as
a property of mind, that it is found in alliance with a
material body ? Surely, if such be the fact, we are at
liberty to declare it. May we then call it a mystery ? In
a certain sense we may. It is a fact isolated and unique.
if we look at matter generally; but it is yet of wide

prevalence, if we combine the number of individuals of the human race with the still greater numbers of the lower animals. The repetition of it over so wide a field redeems the mystery by familiarity; although it does not take away the bold contrast between the animal nature on the one hand, and plants and minerals on the other.

The mystery will be still farther reduced if we can resolve the connexion as stated in gross, to separate and specific laws of connexion. This would be a step of genuine enlightenment in any region of nature. We accept the union as a fact, just as we accept any other union,—Heat with Light, Magnetism with the sesquioxide of iron, Gravity with Inert Matter. We then endeavour to express it in its simplest terms, or under the most comprehensive laws. Let us resolve into the highest possible generalities, the connexion of pleasures and pains with all the physical stimulants of the senses, with all the suggestions of thought, with all the external manifestations in feature, gesture, movement, and secretion; and when this is done we shall have resolved one part of the mystery by the only mode of resolution that the case admits of. Let us go farther if we can : let us generalize the connexions of thought or intellect with nervous and other processes; find out what physical basis specifically belongs to memory, to reason, to imagination, and what are the most general statements of the relationship : we shall then fully, sufficiently, finally explain the alliance of mind and body in the sphere of intellect. There is no other explana-

tion needful, no other competent, no other that would
be explanation. Instead of our being unfortunate, as is
sometimes said, in not being able to know the essence of
either mind or matter, in not rendering an account of their
union, our misfortune would be to have to know anything
different from what we do or may know.   There is surely
nothing to complain of in the circumstance that the elements of our experience are, in the last resort, not one
but *two*. If there were fifty ultimate experiences, none of
them having a single property in common with any other;
and if we had only our present limited powers of understanding, we might be entitled to complain of the world's
mysteriousness, in the one proper acceptation of mystery,
namely, as overpowering our means of intellectual comprehension, as weighing us down with a load of unassimilable
facts. But our actual difficulty is far short of this; the
institution of two distinct entities is not in itself a crushing
dispensation.

It remains to consider the expression most suited to
this union of the two distinct and mutually irresolvable
natures. By inapplicable phraseology many a question
has been darkened and mystified to the point of despair.
In the History of Philosophy we find numerous instances
of contradictions brought about by inappropriate language;
most of all in this very case of mind and body, as will appear
in the closing chapter, on the History of the question.

The doctrine of two substances—a material united

K

with an immaterial in a certain vaguely defined relation
ship—which has prevailed from the time of Thomas
Aquinas to the present day, is now in course of being
modified, at the instance of modern physiology.   The
dependence of purely intellectual operations, as memory,
upon the material processes, has been reluctantly admitted
by the partisans of an immaterial principle ; an admission
incompatible with the isolation of the intellect in Aristotle
and in Aquinas.   This more thorough-going connexion of
the mental and the physical has led to a new form of
expressing the relationship, which is nearer the truth,
without being, in my judgment, quite accurate.   It is now
often said that *the mind and the body act upon each other ;*
that neither is allowed, so to speak, to pursue its course
alone ; there is a constant interference, a mutual influence
between the two.   This view is liable to the following
objections :—

In the first place, it assumes that we are entitled to
speak of mind apart from body, and to affirm its powers
and properties in that separate capacity.   But of mind
apart from body we have no direct experience, and absolutely no knowledge.   The wind may act upon the sea, and
the waves may react upon the wind ; yet the agents are
known in separation, they are seen to exist apart before
the shock of collision ; but we are not allowed to perceive
a mind acting apart from its material companion.

In the second place, we have every reason for believing
that there is, in company with all our mental processes, *an*

unbroken material succession. From the ingress of a sensation, to the outgoing responses in action, the mental succession is not for an instant dissevered from a physical succession. A new prospect bursts upon the view; there is a mental result of sensation, emotion, thought—terminating in outward displays of speech or gesture. Parallel to this mental series is the physical series of facts, the successive agitation of the physical organs, called the eye, the retina, the optic nerve, optic centres, cerebral hemispheres, outgoing nerves, muscles, &c. While we go the round of the mental circle of sensation, emotion, and thought, there is an unbroken physical circle of effects. It would be incompatible with everything we know of the cerebral action, to suppose that the physical chain ends abruptly in a physical void, occupied by an immaterial substance; which immaterial substance, after working alone, imparts its results to the other edge of the physical break, and determines the active response—two shores of the material with an intervening ocean of the immaterial. There is, in fact, no rupture of nervous continuity. The only tenable supposition is, that mental and physical proceed together, as undivided twins. When, therefore, we speak of a mental cause, a mental agency, we have always a *two-sided cause ;* the effect produced is not the effect of mind alone, but of mind in company with body. That mind should have operated on the body, is as much as to say, that a two-sided phenomenon, one side being bodily, can influence the body; it is, after all, body

K 2

acting upon body. When a shock of fear paralyses digestion, it is not the emotion of fear, in the abstract, or as a
pure mental existence, that does the harm; it is the
emotion in company with a peculiarly excited condition of
the brain and nervous system; and it is this condition of
the brain that deranges the stomach. When physical
nourishment, or a physical stimulant, acting through the
blood, quiets the mental irritation, and restores a cheerful
tone, it is not a bodily fact causing a mental fact by a
direct line of causation : the nourishment and the stimulus
determine the circulation of blood to the brain, give a new
direction to the nerve currents; and the mental condition
corresponding to this particular mode of cerebral action
henceforth manifests itself. The line of mental sequence
is thus, not mind causing body, and body causing mind,
but mind-body giving birth to mind-body ; a much more
intelligible position. For this double, or conjoint causation, we can produce evidence ; for the single-handed
causation we have no evidence.

The same line of criticism applies to another phrase
in common use, namely, "the mind uses the body as its
instrument," or medium of operating on the external
world. This also assumes for mind a separate existence,
a power of living apart, an option of working with or
without a body. Actuated by the desire of making itself
known, and of playing a part in the sphere of matter,
the mind uses its bodily ally to gratify this desire; but

if it chose to be self-contained, to live satisfied with its own contemplations, like the gods as conceived by Aristotle, it need not enter into co-operation with any physical process, with brain, senses, or muscular organs. I will not re-iterate the groundlessness of this supposition. The physical alliance is the very law of our mental being; it is not contrived purely for the purpose of making our mental states known: without it we should not have mental states at all. The imparting our feelings to others, and the setting outward things in motion, are consequences of the alliance, but they are not its primary motive. The resolve on our part to affect other minds is already a physical fact, in company with a mental fact; it is not a whit more physical when carried into overt display.

If all mental facts are at the same time physical facts, some will ask what is the meaning of a proper mental fact? Is there any difference at all between mental agents and physical agents? There is a very broad difference, which may be easily illustrated. When any one is pleased, stimulated, cheered, by food, wine, or bracing air—we call the influence physical; it operates on the viscera, and through these upon the nerves, by a chain of sequence purely physical. When one is cheered by good news, by a pleasing spectacle, or by a stroke of success, the influence is mental; sensation, thought, and consciousness are part of the chain; although these

cannot be sustained without their physical basis. The
proper physical fact is a single, one-sided, objective fact;
the mental fact is a two-sided fact,—one of its sides being
a train of feelings, thoughts, or other subjective elements.
We do not fully represent the mental fact, unless we take
account of both the sides. The so-called mental influences,
—cheerful news, a fine poem, and the rest,—cannot
operate, except on a frame physically prepared to respond
to the stimulation.

While admitting that there is something unique, if not
remarkable, in the close incorporation of the two extreme
and contrasted facts, termed Mind and Matter, we must
grant that the total difference of nature has rendered the
union very puzzling to express in language. The history
of the question repeatedly exemplifies this difficulty.

What I have in view is this. When I speak of mind as
allied with body—with a brain and its nerve-currents—I
can scarcely avoid *localizing* the mind, giving it a local
habitation. I am thereupon asked to explain what always
puzzled the schoolmen, namely, whether the mind is all in
every part, or only all in the whole; whether in tapping
any point I may come at consciousness, or whether the
whole mechanism is wanted for the smallest portion of consciousness. One might perhaps turn the question by the
analogy of the telegraph wire, or the electric circuit, and
say that a complete circle of action is necessary to any
mental manifestation; which is probably true. But this

does not meet the case. The fact is, that, all the time that we are speaking of nerves and wires, we are not speaking of mind, properly so called, at all; we are putting forward physical facts that go along with it, but these physical facts are not the mental fact, and they even preclude us from thinking of the mental fact. We are in this fix: mental states and bodily states are utterly contrasted; they cannot be compared, they have nothing in common except the most general of all attributes—degree, and order in time; when engaged with one we must be oblivious of all that distinguishes the other. When I am studying a brain and nerve communications, I am engrossed with properties exclusively belonging to the object or material world; I am unable at that moment (except by very rapid transitions or alternations) to conceive a truly mental fact, my truly mental consciousness. Our mental experience, our feelings and thoughts, have *no extension*, no place, no form or outline, no mechanical division of parts; and we are incapable of attending to anything mental until we shut off the view of all that. Walking in the country in spring, our mind is occupied with the foliage, the bloom, and the grassy meads—all purely objective things: we are suddenly and strongly arrested by the odour of the May-blossom; we give way for a moment to the sensation of sweetness; for that moment the objective regards cease; we think of nothing extended; we are in a state where extension has no footing; there is, to us, place no longer. Such states are of short duration, mere fits, glimpses; they are con-

stantly shifted and alternated with object states, but while
they last and have their full power we are in a different
world ; the material world is blotted out, eclipsed, for the
instant unthinkable. These subject-moments are studied
to advantage in bursts of intense pleasure, or intense pain,
in fits of engrossed reflection, especially reflection upon
mental facts ; but they are seldom sustained in purity
beyond a very short interval ; we are constantly returning
to the object side of things—to the world whose basis is
extension and place.

This, then, as it appears to me, is the only real difficulty
of the physical and mental relationship. There is an
alliance with matter, with the object, or extended world ;
but the thing allied, *the mind proper*, has itself no extension, and cannot be joined in local union. Now, we have
a difficulty in providing any form of language, any familiar
analogy, suited to this unique conjunction ; in comparison
with all ordinary unions, it is a paradox or a contradiction.
We understand union in the sense of local connexion ; here
is a union where local connexion is irrelevant, unsuitable,
contradictory ; for we cannot think of mind without
putting ourselves out of the world of place. When, as in
pure feeling—pleasure or pain—we change from the object
attitude to the subject attitude, we have undergone a
change not to be expressed by place ; the fact is not properly described by the transition from the *external* to the
internal, for that is still a change in the region of the

extended. The only adequate expression is a CHANGE
OF STATE: a change from the state of the extended
cognition to a state of unextended cognition. By various
theologians, heaven has been spoken of as not a place, but
a *state ;* and this is the only phrase that I can find suitable
to describe the vast, though familiar and easy, transition
from the material or extended, to the immaterial or unextended side of our being.

When, therefore, we talk of incorporating mind with
brain, we must be held as speaking under an important
reserve or qualification. Asserting the union in the
strongest manner, we must yet deprive it of the almost
invincible association of *union in place.* An extended
organism is the condition of our passing into a state where
there is no extension. A human being is an extended and
material mass, attached to which is the power of becoming
alive to feeling and thought, the extreme remove from all
that is material; a condition of *trance* wherein, while it
lasts, the material drops out of view—so much so, that we
have not the power to represent the two extremes as lying
side by side, as container and contained, or in any other
mode of local conjunction. The condition of our existing
thoroughly in the one, is the momentary eclipse or extinction of the other.

The only mode of union that is not contradictory is the
union of close succession in *time;* or of position in a continued thread of conscious life. We are entitled to say

that the same being is, by alternate fits, object and subject, under extended and under unextended consciousness;
and that without the extended consciousness the unextended would not arise. Without certain peculiar modes
of the extended—what we call a cerebral organization,
and so on—we could not have those times of trance, our
pleasures, our pains, and our ideas, which at present we
undergo fitfully and alternately with our extended
consciousness.

CHAPTER VII.

HISTORY OF THE THEORIES OF THE SOUL.

LET me first classify the different views that may be held as to the ultimate component elements of a human being.

I. TWO SUBSTANCES.

1. *Both Material.*

a. The prevailing conception among the lower races.
b. Most of the ancient Greek philosophers.
c. The early Christian Fathers.

2. *An Immaterial and a Material.*

a. Commencement in Plato and in Aristotle.
b. The later Fathers from the age of Augustine.
c. The Schoolmen.
d. Descartes.
e. The prevalent opinion.

II. ONE SUBSTANCE.

1. *Mind and Matter the same.*

a. The cruder forms and expressions of Materialism.
b. The Pantheistic Idealism of Fichte.

2. *Contrast of Mind and Matter saved.*

Guarded or qualified Materialism—held by many Physiologists and Metaphysicians : the growing opinion.

As the present historical sketch is principally occupied with (1) the development, and (2) the decay of Immaterialism, let me further prepare the way by a summary view of the arguments of its supporters, which are also the points of attack of its assailants.

1. The Soul must partake of the nature or essence of the Deity.

2. The Soul has no determinate place in the body.

3. Reason or Thought—the power of cognizing the Universal—is incompatible with matter (Aquinas).

4. The dignity of the Soul requires an essence superior to matter.

5. Matter is divisible; Mind indivisible.

6. Matter is changeable and corruptible ; Mind is a pure substance.

7. Mind is active, or possesses Force ; Matter is passive, inert, the thing acted on.

8. The Soul is the primary source or principle of Life.

9. The Mind has a Personal Identity ; the particles of the Body are continually changing.

The interesting and elaborate inquiries, recently prosecuted with regard to the mental condition and modes of thinking of the Lower Races, have contributed the first chapter of the history of the soul.   I allude more particularly to the writings of Sir John Lubbock, Mr. McLennan, and Mr. Tylor, who have thrown a flood of light on the primitive history of mankind; bringing the development of religious ideas up to the point where Greek philosophy took its start.

Mr. Tylor has appropriated the word "Animism" to express the recognition, throughout all the races of mankind, of the Soul as a distinct entity.   There are two classes of souls: those of individual creatures, like ourselves, capable of continued existence after death; and those of purely spiritual beings of all grades up to the most powerful deities.

As regards our present subject, two distinct problems (says Mr. Tylor) engaged the thoughts of men at a low level of culture. First, What makes the difference between a living body and a dead one—between one awake and one either asleep or in some lifeless condition? Secondly, What are those human shapes appearing in dreams and visions?   In early savage philosophy, the two sets of phenomena were made to account for and implement each other, by the conception of an *apparition-soul* or a ghost-soul. The absence of this constitutes the lifeless body; its presence as a visitor made the dream, apparition, or ghost.

The matter, material, or substance of the ghost-soul is a sort of vapour, film, or shadow, impalpable to the touch, and invisible, except on the particular occasions when it manifests itself in dream or vision; exercising physical power; bearing a likeness to the person that it belongs to, and showing itself clad in habiliments and accoutrements; capable not only of leaving the body, but of flashing swiftly from place to place, with a perfect mastery of distance; able to take possession of the bodies of other men, or of animals, and to act through these. As a matter of course, the soul is the principle of life and of all mental activity in the individual that it primarily belongs to. (Tylor, "Primitive Culture," I. 387).*

The words for expressing the soul show the prevailing conception of its nature or substance. Foremost among these is the "shadow" or "shade," so widely diffused

---

* The possession of a Soul was not limited to human beings. That Animals also had souls was an equally prevalent belief, and was the foundation of numerous rites and customs. No radical distinction could be drawn between men and animals, as to the possession of the attributes grouped together under the Soul.

The analogy between men and Plants is much feebler; but it still contains the marked features of life and death, health and sickness. This was enough for endowing Plants too with souls. The doctrine of transmigration allows plants to enter into the line of successive tenancy of a spirit. Moreover, the existence of tree-worship carries with it by inference the belief in tree-souls.

The attributing of spirits, or souls, to Inanimate objects would seem to proceed upon a very attenuated analogy. In the case of great natural agents, as the winds, the rivers, the oceans, fire, the sun, the circumstance of exercising power is itself a strong point of resemblance, although accompanied with great disparity; the personifying of nature has here its commencement. The so-called object-souls, souls of useful articles—tools, implements, armour, houses, canoes—have a place among the spirits of the inferior races: a purely utilitarian conception of the soul. The often-cited worship of "stocks and stones" is no doubt the lowest degradation of the human faculty of reverence; but the reason of its existence has been assigned with great probability. (Sir John Lubbock, "Origin of Civilization," chap v.)

among civilized languages. The "shadow" happily combined two of the requisites of the soul, the *unsubstantial
quality*, and the *form* of the individual man ; although, if
critically considered, it would have various drawbacks.
Next comes the "heart," from the connexion of the pulses
with full vitality: allied to which is the widely-spread
identity of soul and "blood." Thirdly, great use has
been made of the "breath" in designating the soul ; the
connexion of breathing with life being obvious; *psyche,
pneuma, animus, spiritus*, are of this origin ; and there
are parallels in the Semitic and other languages. The
association of life with the "pupil of the eye," has also
been traced in various traditions, European and others;
from the marked difference between the eye in full health
and animation, and its appearance in sickness and in
death. (Tylor, pp. 388—391.)*

Thus, we may very fairly say that the sole theory
of mind and body existing in the lower stages of culture,
is a *double materialism*. This was within their grasp.
An Immaterial soul was entirely beyond their intellectual
comprehension. Until the Greek philosophy taught the
world how to use and abuse abstract notions, Immaterialism was not an attainable phase of thought.

In turning next, therefore, to the speculations of Ancient

* Mr. Tylor traces an interesting result of the plurality of figurative
designations for the soul, in the development of a plurality of functions,
and even a *plurality of souls;* so early did the ambiguities and confusions of language govern men's conceptions of things.

Greece, we are greatly helped by the well wrought-out delineation of the theories that first constituted the education of the Grecian thinkers. The bold originality and intellectual acumen of the Greeks were displayed in this, as in so many other fields; but they could not entirely free themselves of their inherited bias.

Generally speaking, the Greek philosophers were double materialists. They duly distinguished between the substance of the soul and the substance of the body; but the substance of the soul was still accounted matter—namely, the two higher elements, Air and Fire; to which Aristotle, subtilizing still farther, added an Æther, or fifth essence (quintessence). These higher elements made up the celestial bodies, as well as the gods themselves; they were distinguished from the lower couple, Earth and Water, not merely by their subtle and impalpable consistency, but by the regularity and perfection of their movements; the gross matter below the sphere of the moon was subject to great irregularity, and was on that account an inferior essence. It was not to be expected that the substance of the human soul would transcend the substance of the gods; the assimilation of mind to Deity is common at all stages of culture.

We perceive from this summary view, which will presently be unfolded into details, that the ancient Greeks made a step in advance of the earlier races, by availing themselves of their new physical speculations, whereby they classified the great elements,—Earth, Water, &c.—and

distinguished the several characteristics of these. From the "shadow" of the primitive thinker to the Air and Fire of the Grecian sage, there was a great stride in refinement of conception, although there was no essential departure from a materialistic theory.

The ancients differed from the moderns in not admitting the *separate* existence of the soul (although Aquinas understood Plato's pre-existence as separation). Those of them that held the doctrine of personal immortality coupled it with transmigration; the soul in quitting one body found another ready for its reception. After-existence was thus coupled with pre-existence. It was repugnant to these philosophers to suppose an absolute beginning, or creation, either for matter or for mind.

Let us, however, descend to particulars.

The pre-Socratic philosophers made very little way with the nature of the Soul. Several of them touched the subject, and brought it under their peculiar scheme of nature in general. HERACLEITUS adopted the principle of *Mutation* as his basis of explanation of all things; and the Soul partook of the common attribute in a higher degree. Its subtlety and fluency enabled it to know all other things. EMPEDOCLES is the originator of the doctrine of the *Four Elements*—fire, air, water, earth; with Love and Hatred as principles of motion, the one uniting and the other disjoining the elements. The Soul is compounded in the same way; and on the principle of like being known

L

by like, each of its elements knows the like element in the world. ANAXAGORAS set up *Nous* or *Mind* as the great prime mover of the world. While all material bodies were mixtures of *all* the simple elements, Nous was the pure, unmixed element; the thinnest and subtlest of all matter, more so than either air or fire, but of great energy: unacted on by matter, it was itself not only cognitive, but active, and the source of all change. DIOGENES, of Apollonia, adopted *Air* as the constituent of the soul, at once mobile, all penetrating and intelligent. DEMOKRITUS, the *Atomist*, gave to the element fire, and to the soul, the atoms of spherical figure; it was their nature never to be at rest: they were the sources of all motion.

PYTHAGORAS had called the soul a Number and a Harmony, like everything else; but some of the Pythagoreans looked upon it as an aggregate of particles of extreme subtlety, pervading the air, and in constant agitation.

In these views we see two distinct tendencies:—to regard the soul as subtle, *ethereal*, and refined, in contrast with the grossness of solid matter; and to view it as the *active* principle of nature, as self-moved, and the cause of motion in corporeal things.

PLATO's theory of the Soul was one of the influences determining the modern settlement of the question. It starts from his doctrine of eternal, self-existent Ideas or Forms, which were anterior to what we call the universe, or the Kosmos. To the formation of the Kosmos, there concurred two factors,—the Ideas and a co-eternal Chaos, or indeterminate matter, in discordant and irregular motion. A Divine Architect, or Demiurgus, on contemplating the Ideas, made the world in conformity therewith, so far as the things of sense could be made to correspond with the eternal types. The Architect had to contend with a pre-existing power, called Necessity, represented by the irregular motions of the primitive chaos; only up to a certain point could he control this Necessity, and make it give place to regularity. With such a difficulty to struggle against, the Demiurgus proceeds to construct or fabricate the Kosmos. In its totality this is a vast and comprehensive animated being; the model for it is the Idea of Animal,—the Self-Animal (αὐτόζωον). As created, the Kosmos is a scheme of rotatory spheres, and has both a Soul and a Body. The Soul, rooted at the centre, and pervading the whole, is *self-moving*, and the cause of movement in the Kosmical Body. The Kosmos, in its peripheral or celestial regions, contains the gods; in its central or lower regions of air, water, and earth, are placed men, quadrupeds, birds, and fishes. From the Divine part of the Kosmos there was a gradual degeneracy in the creation of men and animals. The human cranium was a little Kosmos, containing a rational and immortal soul, of adulterated materials; while in the body there are two inferior and mortal souls: the higher of the two situated in the chest, and manifesting

Energy, courage, anger, &c. ; the lower placed in the abdomen, and displaying Appetite. The two lower souls are the disturbers of the higher rational soul, confusing its rotations, and perverting their harmonious properties. Yet notwithstanding its superior dignity, the soul is never detached from the body; it has the corporeal properties of extension and movement ; and it is the moving power of the whole system.

In comparison with the loftiness and purity of the Eternal Ideas, the Kosmical Soul itself was but an imperfect mixture, or compromise between the Ideal and the Sensible ; and the human Soul could be no better. Still, in its participation of the Ideas (although conjoined with sense), it was self-moving and immortal.

ARISTOTLE set himself to confute all previous theories of the Soul. He rejected the doctrine of self-motion as the property of Soul; he regarded as untenable the favourite theory of perception—" Like is known only by like"—and advanced very pertinent objections to that view. As to self-motion, he considered it incorrect to say that the soul is moved at all ; looking more especially at the intellect or Nous, we might rather say that the state is not movement, but rest or suspension of movement.

Both in his criticism and in his constructive theories, Aristotle made an advance upon his predecessors. His eye for facts, and his sobriety of judgment, raised him above fanciful and one-sided vagaries. He had studied the actual phenomena of living bodies; had meditated deeply on the wide chasm that divides the inanimate from the animate world; animated beings as a whole were to his mind more completely separated from inorganic bodies as a whole, than animals were separated from plants.

But it was the characteristic of this extraordinary genius to work at both ends of the scientific process; he was alike a devotee to facts, and a master of the highest abstractions. In this last capacity he originated many of the subtle distinctions that have ever since permeated human thought.

Whoever would begin at the beginning of Aristotle's philosophy must first master his Four Causes, or conditions of all production :—(1) *Matter*, the material cause, what anything is made of—marble, brass, wood, &c.; (2) *Form*, the formal cause, the type, plan, or design of the maker—the idea of the statuary, the working plans of the architect; (3) the *Efficient* cause, or prime mover—human muscle, water, wind, or whatever is the force employed; (4) the *Final* cause, the end or purpose of the workman—his pleasure, profit, fame.

Having once seen the scope of these four exhaustive conditions of every work of human industry, the reader may let drop the two last, as of far inferior importance, and concentrate his attention upon the distinction between the two first—Matter and Form, which, more than any of his other distinctions, lies at the root of Aristotle's general

thinking. He expands and diversifies the contrast in end-
less ways. We must observe, however, that Matter, as one of
the Four Causes, is not without Form, in the literal sense ;
a block of marble has its form, although not the form
intended ultimately. Now there is some ground for
supposing that Aristotle, in pushing the distinction to the
logical point of *two abstractions,*—an abstract matter and
an abstract form, separable in reasoning, but inseparable
in reality,—had still clinging to him the original contrast
of *rough unshaped* matter, and the *finished production* of
the workman. At all events, his account of an individual
substance is to regard (1) the Form, (2) the Matter, (3)
the Compound of the two.

That he was unduly possessed with the distinction
between formed matter and raw material, to the obscuring
of the logical distinction, we may infer from his making
out a difference of dignity between form and matter.
Form is the higher, grander, more perfect entity ; Matter
has only a second place. This remark is entirely out of
place in the logical distinction between the form of a brass
ring, and the matter of it (abstracted from the form).

Matter may be body, but it is not necessarily body. It
is intelligible only as the correlate of Form. Each variety
of matter has its appropriate form, and each variety of
form its appropriate matter. There are gradations in
matter, from the first matter (materia prima), which has no
Form at all, to the highest developments which approach
near to pure Form. The only meaning we can give to

these last statements, is to suppose that he had in his mind the different stages of elaboration of the material of the globe, from a so-called shapeless mass of mud, to the consummate organization of a living being.

Another distinction struck out and designated by Aristotle, and permanently retained from its corresponding to a difference in the nature of things, was the distinction of *Potential* and *Actual*. Active agents have moments of rest or remission ; they possess power, but do not use it. The eye awake is actually engaged in seeing ; in sleep, it is not deprived of the power, but holds it unemployed. Some form of language was required to discriminate the situation of having power in reserve and quiescence from total want of power ; Great Britain, in time of peace, is not to be confounded with nations destitute of a navy.

The distinction of Potential and Actual serves its own turn in its own way, and has no connection with the other great distinction. But Aristotle could not help mixing up the two ; he sees in Matter by itself the Potential, in the imparting of Form to matter, the Actual or full reality. There is here apparently a reference to the distinction of the two causes. Matter in the rough is still a compound of matter and form ; a block of marble from the quarries is no more devoid of form, in the logical view, than a slab in the frieze of the Parthenon. The transition from the Potential to the Actual as regards bodies, is a transition

from one Form to another Form.   Still, for understanding
what follows, we must keep in view the identifying of
Actuality with Form in the sense of some superior
product of formed material.

We are now to see how he applied these rather shaky
distinctions to the great problem of Soul and Body.

In the antithesis of Matter and Form—Potential and
Actual, the soul ranks not with matter but with Form,
not with the potential but with the Actual.   It has
Matter (the Body) as its correlate; and this matter is
highly organized, in other words, fitted with capacities
or potentialities, and to these the Soul is the complement.
The implication of Potential Matter and Actualizing
Form or Soul is the totality of the living being.   In his
fondness for carrying out distinctions, Aristotle remarks
that the living being has its two conditions of dormancy
and full exercise, and the first or lowest stage of Actuality
is quite enough to distinguish it; the second or higher
Actuality, therefore, need not be introduced into the
definition.   Accordingly the Soul stands thus: — "The
first actuality (entelechy) of a natural organized body,
having life in potentiality."

The strong point of the definition is the closeness of the
connection of Mind and Body.   Indeed they are too
closely connected; or rather the manner of their connexion
is incorrectly stated.   In point of fact, the two are not
relative and correlative, like Form and Matter (logically

viewed). Of correlative couples,—as light-dark, up-down,
cause-effect, parent-child, ruler-subject, supporting-sup-
ported,—the one can in no sense subsist without the
other ; the existence of either by itself is a contradiction
in terms ; a parent without a child, a thing supporting
with nothing to support—are absurd and unmeaning.
Now, although, in reality, there is a close alliance between
Soul and Body, there would not be a self-contradiction in
supposing them separate; for anything we can see, the
body might have its bodily functions without the soul, and
the soul might have its psychical functions in some other
connexion than our present bodies. Indeed, Aristotle
himself reserves a certain portion of the Soul for independent existence. We must, therefore, pronounce the
comparison of Soul and Body to a correlated couple, as
irrelevant and unsuitable.*

Nevertheless, out of the alleged mutual implication of
the two, Aristotle obtains a very felicitous observation.
All the actions and passions of the mind, he says, have two
sides—a formal side as regards the soul, and a material side
as regards the body. It is the business of two different
sets of inquirers to master these two sides. The
physical philosopher (ὁ φυσικός) and the mental philosopher would view the same passions differently. Take,

* In a passing illustration of dialectical method. (Topics, Book V.),
Aristotle speaks of the soul as exercising command, the body as obeying
command. This is a familiar enough mode of representing the relation
of the two, but it has no scientific validity. The power commanding is
not pure, but embodied mind.

for example, the passion of Anger. According to the mental philosopher, anger is the appetite for injuring some one (a truly *mental* fact). According to the physical philosopher, it is a boiling up of blood about the heart, with increase of animal heat (*physical* circumstances). Now, this illustration is perfect as representing the two sets of facts, different and yet inseparable. It was, however, but a casual glimpse, a mere incidental flash in a prevailing gloom. His attempt to carry out the illustration to intellectual states, as memory, merely leads to some correct remarks as to the necessity of a sound condition of the sentient organs and body generally, in order to the exercise of intelligence.

Other modes are given for stating the implication or correlation. The Soul is the *cause* and principle of a living body. Of the Four Causes, the body furnishes the Material, and the soul comprises all the three remaining, Formal, Movent or Efficient, Final.

So much for one phase of the Aristotelian doctrine—the mode of stating the Union of the soul with the body. The other phase respects the gradation of Souls—a succession of Nutrient, Sentient, Intelligent principles.

The remark has already been made that Aristotle had something like an adequate sense of the difference between Inanimate matter and Living bodies. As, perhaps, the earliest scientific naturalist, he perceived that the living body was characterised by organization, and by the possession of remarkable powers or functions. He did not so strongly realize the boundary between life without consciousness (as in Plants) and life with consciousness (in Animals and Man). Hence he treated as generically homogeneous all living functions, all the active powers belonging to organized individuals. He applied the higher term "Soul" (ψυχή) to all the characteristic functions of living bodies, from nutrition up to the loftiest attributes of intellect.*

Accordingly, we must start from the *Nutritive* Soul, the basis of all the others, the first constituent of the living individual, the implication of Form with Matter in a body organized as a nutritive body; the soul of digestion, nutrition, and propagation of the species. Like all Soul (as will be seen) it partakes of the Celestial Heat, through which animated bodies possess their warmth.

From the nutritive we pass to the higher soul, both nutritive and *Sentient*. Herein lies the characteristic superiority of the Animal to the Plant. There is a great advance in point of dignity, as we may suppose. Applying the universal solvent—Form *versus* Matter—we are to remark that the soul as sentient and percipient, receives the *form* of the thing perceived without the matter; which is to beg the whole question of External Perception. Nevertheless, Aristotle's discussion of the Senses and

* Mr Tylor would say that the Plant-Soul of Aristotle was the survival of the Plant-Soul of the lower races, rather than his own independent reflections on the community of plants and animals as living things.

Sensation at large is full of just and original remarks, and was a real contribution to Psychology.

From the Sentient Soul, we pass to the *Noëtic*, the Nous, or Intelligence. The drawing of too sharp a line between Sense and Intelligence has been the fruitful source of confusions in philosophy; and has lent itself to the doctrine of the Immaterial Soul. At the same time, Aristotle fully recognizes the dependence of intellect upon sensation; we cannot cogitate or reason without sensible images (phantasms). But to reconcile this with the views that he took of the special grandeur and *isolation* of the Nous, was beyond his might. He declares (against his own definition of the Soul) that the noëtic function has no bodily organs, that it is Form, pure and simple (seeming to contradict farther the mutual relationship of Form and Matter).

At this point, however, he looks out for a new ally. The scene changes from earth to heaven. The human soul is not to be finished without celestial fire.

The grand region of Form (pure and unadulterated) is the CELESTIAL BODY, the entire concave of heaven, with its eternal rotations, the abode of all divine natures, comprising the invisible gods, and the sun, moon, and stars. From this celestial region proceeds all life, all force; to every Soul, every Form that animates the matter of a living body, it imparts its vital properties. It is needless to comment farther on the self-contradictory employment of the abstraction, Form, to signify the heavenly sub-

stance.   Aristotle's Physics and Astronomy were his
weakest parts, and laid him open to the merciless scourge
of Galileo.   Even there he is not without brilliant
inspirations; but he is led captive, with the vulgar, by
the enchantment of distance.

The Nous emanated from a peculiar and select influence
of the celestial body; and its own operations are correspondingly dignified.   It cognizes the abstract and the
universal.   It has two modes or degrees, on which hang
great issues.   There is, on the one hand, the receptive
Intellect, *Intellectus Patiens*, and, on the other, the
constructive or reproductive Intellect, *Intellectus Agens*
(νοῦς θεορητικός); the first perishes with the body; the
second, the *Agens*, is intellectual energy, in the purest
manifestation, separable from the animal body, and
immortal.   The climax is now reached; logical consistency
is abandoned; and there is gained a transcendental
starting-point for the Immaterialism of after ages.

Of the best known Greek sects, the Epicureans denied
altogether the survival of the soul.   The Stoics affirmed
the soul as well as the body to be material, and considered
it a detached fragment of the all-pervading soul of the
world, into which, after the death of the individual, it was
re-absorbed.

Our course takes us next to the Fathers of the Christian Church.

The early Fathers had been pagan philosophers before they were Christians; they thus brought with them into Christianity more or less of the tenets of their respective philosophical sects. Accordingly, the double materialism of antiquity was a prevailing tenet down to the fifth century. A proper immaterial or spiritual substance, as recognized by us, was as yet incomprehensible to the greater number of men. Such a thing, no doubt, had made a beginning in the Greek schools, but was not as yet fully formed even there; and it received no aid, either from Judaism or from Christianity. In these early centuries, it was very generally held as essential to the Christian doctrine of future rewards and punishments, that mind should be a corporeal substance; for only matter could be susceptible to physical pain and pleasure.

In general, we may say, that the early Fathers, whether accepting the Oriental and Greek notions of transmigration and pre-existence, or, like Irenæus and Arnobius, making the immortality of the soul depend upon the will of God in his purposes for the salvation of part of mankind, describe in nearly the same terms the essence of Deity and the essence of the soul. Before and even after the Nicene Council, God was often described as a "sublime light." A converted Epicurean would add to this a human form; a Platonist would use the term "incorporeal" in the Platonic sense of the word, which was not the modern sense.

From Dr. Donaldson's History of Christian Doctrine

may be gleaned the views on the Soul held by the
Fathers of the *second century*, named the APOLOGISTS.
They were influenced by Platonic philosophy much less
than is generally supposed. The only Platonist among
them was Athenagoras. They were much more influenced
by the prevailing materialistic tendencies; Stoicism being
what might be called the established religion of the time.
Justin Martyr's expressions on the nature of God and
the Soul are indefinite, but he would not seem to have
recognized wholly immaterial spirit : although he rejects
the Anthropomorphism of the Jews, he ascribes to God
shape and locality; and though nowhere definite on the
state of the soul after death, he considers it heresy to
say that the soul is taken up to heaven ; and he holds
that men rise with the same bodies. Tatian, however,
the pupil of Justin, both is more definite, and recognizes
a wholly immaterial spirit conjoined with a material spirit
in the human body; God is immaterial, fleshless, and
bodiless. His doctrine is, that there are two spirits in
the universe, manifesting themselves in individual varieties
of form ; at one time they lived in union, but the lower
spirit (the soul) became disobedient, fled from the perfect
spirit, and sought a baser fellowship with matter; yet
after all, when re-united as in man with the higher spirit,
it becomes immortal. Theophilus does not maintain the
immateriality of God ; he only holds with Justin that
the form of God cannot be expressed. Athenagoras
differed essentially from his contemporaries in regard to

the nature of the soul: he does not mention *Pneuma*, or higher Spirit; and he speaks of the soul as purely spiritual, though with a spirituality liable to be disturbed by its material tendencies.

CLEMENT of Alexandria speaks thus of God:—"A positive knowledge of God is impossible: we know only what he is not. He is formless and nameless, though we are right to call him by the noblest names. He is infinite; he is neither Genus, nor Differentia, nor Species, nor Individual, nor Number, nor Accident, nor anything that any positive attribute can be ascribed to." This is certainly not Corporeality, neither is it what we mean by an Incorporeal nature. It is merely working up a powerful impression, by the rhetorical employment of negatives.

ORIGEN conceived of God as a purely spiritual being,—not fire, not light, not æther, but an absolutely incorporeal Unity or monad. Only on the supposition of Incorporeality can he be considered absolutely unchangeable, for everything material is changeable, divisible, transitory. This is an obvious following out of the transcendental germs in Greek philosophy. "In the world, God, who is himself unextended, is everywhere present by his active power, like the builder in his work, or as our soul, in its sensitive part, is spread through the whole body; only he does not fill evil with his presence." "The human soul, as a created spirit, was enclosed in matter because of sin." With all this, Origen further remarks that the word "incorporeal" is not to be found in Scripture, and that a *spirit* strictly means a body.

TERTULLIAN is represented (by Ueberweg) as joining, in the manner of the Stoics, with an Ethics tending to the repression of sense, a sensationalist doctrine of cognition, and a materialistic Psychology. He is a coarse Realist. "The senses deceive not: all that is real is body. The corporeality of God does not, however, detract from his sublimity, nor that of the soul from its immortality. Everything that is, is body after its kind. The Deity is a very pure luminous air, diffused everywhere. What is not body is nothing. Who shall deny that God is body, though he is a spirit? A spirit is a body of its own kind, in its own form. *The soul has the human form, the same as its body, only it is delicate, clear, and ethereal.* Unless it were corporeal, how could it" (as the Stoics also said) "be affected by the body, be able to suffer or be nourished within the body?" "Man is made in the likeness of God; God, in forming the first man, took for pattern the future man Christ."

The materialism of Tertullian is thus pronounced and decisive. Then, again, Melito wrote a treatise to prove God's corporeality. Gregory Nazianzen conceives of spirit as possessing only the properties of motion and diffusion. Maximus could not accept the immensity of God, because he did not see how two substances could exist together in the same space. Even when the Deity was called

M

incorporeal, this property was not incompatible with visibility under certain circumstances; it meant only a negation, somewhat in the manner of the ancients, of the grosser properties of matter. That spirits could be seen was a very common belief; many persons declared that they had seen the souls of the dying as they left the body. Gradually, however, the attribute of visibility was abstracted from the nature of spirit; and the Deity began to be considered incorporeal, meaning also invisible; but the human soul did not rise at once to the same august distinction. Thus in Origen, the soul would seem to have a middle place between gross matter and the one truly spiritual essence—the Deity. It is to him a matter of astonishment that the *material* soul should have ideas of immaterial things; and he concludes that it must possess, if not an absolute, at least a relative immateriality.

So much for the double materialism prevailing among the early Fathers. We shall next see the beginning of the spiritualistic movement within the Church. At this point, however, we may bring in the Neo-Platonists, who represent the closing influence of Pagan philosophy, and acted perceptibly on the later Fathers and the Schoolmen.

PLOTINUS (204—269, A.D.) agrees with Plato in the grand distinction of the Ideal and the Sensible, and in attributing to the soul an intermediate nature. He differs from Plato with regard to the relation of the Ideas to the One or the Good. While in the Platonic system the One or the Good is included as the highest among the Ideas, and all the Ideas are considered to have independent existence,—iu Neo-Platonism, it is elevated above the Ideas, and is made the source whence they emanate.

The One or the Good is the primary essence, the original unity, from which all things have sprung. It is neither Nous or Reason, nor anything cognized by Reason; for each of these necessarily implies the other; and the nature of the primary essence, as absolute unity, forbids its being identified with anything implying duality. Things emanate from the One, as rays emanate from the sun. The direct product of the One is the Nous, which is an image of it. The image involuntarily turns towards its original in order to behold it, and, through this act of comprehending what is supra-sensible, it becomes Nous. In the Nous the Ideas are immanent, not as mere thoughts, but as its component parts.

The Soul is an image and product of the Nous, as the Nous is of the One; and it also in its turn produces the corporeal. It is turned partly to the Nous as its producer, and partly to the corporeal, its product. There is, therefore, in the Soul an Ideal indivisible element, and a divisible element, from which the material world is produced. The Soul is an Immaterial substance. It is not a body, nor is it inseparable from a body; for not only the Nous, its

highest principle, but even memory, perception, and the
vegetative force are separable from the body. The body
is in the Soul, not the Soul in the body. Thus a portion
of the Soul is without any body; and for the functions
of this portion the co-operation of the body is entirely
unnecessary. Even the faculties of sense are not *contained in* the body; they are only *present with* it,
as forces given by the Soul to the various organs for the
discharge of their functions. The whole Soul is present
not only in the whole body, but also in each separate
part, not being divided among the members; it is *entirely
present in the whole, and entirely in every part.* In
one sense, indeed, the Soul is divided, since it is in all
parts of the body; but in each of these parts it is present
as a whole.

Here we perceive a distinct advance towards Immaterialism. In the Neo-Platonic doctrines are to be found
the germs of various ideas that afterwards played a
prominent part in the present subject. That the lower
powers of mind and life are separable from the body,
and that the body is contained in the soul, are tenets
reproduced in the subsequent development of the subject.
The notion that the whole soul is in the whole body
and in every part, was taken up by Augustine, then by
Claudian Mamertus, and from them passed over to the
Schoolmen, with whom it was a favourite maxim.

We now proceed to the later Fathers. The spiritualistic

movement may be said to be headed by St. Augustine, the most profound and metaphysical of all the Latin Fathers; by Claudian Mamertus, a priest of Vienne, in the south of France; and in Asia, by Nemesius, Bishop of Emesa.

But even anterior to Augustine (354—430), there were indications of the coming change. In this view, Gregory of Nyssa (331—394) is of importance. His work on the Creation of Man (says Ueberweg) contains a number of psychological remarks. Scriptural views are mixed up with Platonic and Aristotelian opinions. The possibility of the creation of matter, by the Divine Spirit, depends upon its being the unity of qualities in themselves immaterial. The human spirit interpenetrates the whole body; it came into existence with the body, and neither before nor after it. *The spirituality of God, which is beyond dispute,* proves the possibility of immaterial existence. The soul is a created, living, thinking, and (so long as it is provided with organs of sense) percipient entity. The thinking power does not belong to matter; otherwise *matter generally would exhibit it* [a happy hit], and in consequence would assume a variety of artificial forms.

In AUGUSTINE's discussion of this subject, the most remarkable point is his clear conception of the contrast between the respective properties of matter and of mind. He maintains that such attributes as length, breadth,

depth, hardness, &c., are attributes only of matter, and
are unintelligible when applied to mind. "The soul
must not be conceived as in any way long, or broad, or
strong. These are corporeal properties, and so we are
inquiring about the soul after the manner of bodies" (De
Quant. Animæ, cap. 3.). Thus while other qualities, such
as hardness and colour, are occasionally mentioned,
extension is always recognized as the great distinctive
attribute of matter.

On this definition of matter Augustine founds his proofs
of the soul's immateriality. It does not possess this
characteristic property of matter, and therefore it cannot
be material. This position he very often states and
defends. His principal arguments are drawn from the
superiority of the soul to the body, from the nature of
consciousness and of memory, and from the equal presence
of the soul in every part of the body.

The soul is Superior to the body. From it alone are
derived life, movement, and sensation, none of which are
possessed by the body after the soul has fled. Thus the
soul, though working through bodily organs, must be, in
its own nature, superior to the body it animates. It is
invisible, incorporeal, spiritual.

Several arguments are drawn from our Consciousness of
mental states. The soul, he says, is known by us directly.
Our thoughts, desires, knowledge, ignorance, are better
known than the objects around us, since these last are
perceived through the medium of bodily organs. If, then,

the soul be corporeal, it must be known to us as such. Yet in this direct knowledge of it we have no cognizance of corporeal qualities, such as size, shape, or colour ; and hence Augustine concludes that no such qualities belong to it. Moreover, while we positively *know* that thinking and feeling are properties of the soul, we can only *suppose* that it is a material substance. That we have no real knowledge of such a substance is proved by the variety of conjectures about its nature. If we separate what we really *know* from what we only *think*, there remain such properties as life, thought, and feeling, which none have ever doubted.

Another argument is founded on the nature of Memory. In the mind are stored up the images of a great variety of material objects. Though the body is small, the mind can take in the images of the widest domains; "and that it is not diffused through the places is shown by this, that it is not as it were comprehended by the images of the greatest places, but rather comprehends them, not by any enclosing (*non sine aliquo*), but by a certain indescribable power " (Contra Epist. Manich., cap. 17.). If, then, these images, which resemble bodies, are really incorporeal, we cannot believe otherwise of what has no appearance of corporeal properties. And if the things contained in the mind are immaterial, so also is the mind itself.

Augustine lays considerable stress on the Neo-Platonic subtlety that the whole soul is at the same time in

every part of the body. "The soul is at the same time
wholly present not only in the entire mass of the body,
but also in every particle of it" (De Immort. Animæ,
cap. 16.). "When there is any pain in the foot, the
eye looks, the tongue speaks, the hand moves; and
this would not occur unless what of the soul is in
those parts felt also in the foot; nor if not present in
the foot could it feel what has there happened " (Id. ib.).
And this presence of the whole soul in every part of
the body is not similar to the diffusion of bodies through
space; for these are larger or smaller according to the
space occupied. Nor is it like the case of a quality,
such as whiteness, being wholly present in every part
of some concrete object; for the matter that is white
in one part has no connexion with the whiteness in
any other part. Wherefore the soul possesses a peculiar
nature of its own, having qualities exhibited by no
material substance.

In addition to these general arguments, Augustine
brings forward special considerations to prove the
immateriality of the rational soul. The objects of the
Reason are incorporeal. The images of corporeal things,
which it compares and judges, though resembling matter,
are really unextended, and therefore immaterial. Truth
and wisdom, which are perceived by the reason, have
no trace of material properties. Nor in the faculty
itself can we detect any such attributes. It cannot
be divided into parts and extended through space in

the manner of bodies. From all this, therefore, it is concluded that the rational soul is not material.

In answer to the objection that, if the soul has no length, breadth, or thickness, it must be nothing, Augustine maintains that there are many really existing things that have none of these qualities. Justice, for example, has no extension, and yet it is not merely a real thing, but is of a higher nature than any corporeal object. The Deity is also without these attributes; and whoever believes the soul to be corporeal ought in consistency to hold the same opinion of God. The want of such properties, therefore, really proves the soul to be of higher dignity and value.

Since, then, the soul is not matter, it may be asked by what name we are to call it. Augustine replies that " whatever is not matter and yet has real existence, is properly termed *spirit*" (De Quant. Animæ, cap. 13). This, he says, is supported by the usage of Scripture, though the word is also applied there to the intellectual part alone.

Having drawn so broad a contrast between mind and matter, Augustine felt the standing difficulty of conceiving how the immaterial soul can act on the matter of the body in producing movement. Hence he thought that the soul does not act directly on the denser parts of the body, but on a corporeal substance nearer in its nature to the incorporeal. This substance he calls light and air, and supposes that these are mingled

through the denser materials. The commands of the
soul are first communicated to this more subtle matter,
and by it are immediately conveyed to the heavier
elements.

As regards the immortality of the soul, Augustine holds
that no created being can be immortal in the same sense
as God, since the existence of every creature depends continually on the Divine will.   At the same time he maintains that none of the changes we see occurring either in
the soul itself or in the body, tend towards the destruction
of the soul. Even matter is not destroyed by change :
however the form may be altered, it is still matter as
much as before. And if such is the case with corporeal
things, we cannot suppose that in this point the soul is
inferior to them, since mind of any sort is superior to all
material objects. Still farther, he reasons that the soul
cannot be destroyed by any other created being, whether
corporeal or spiritual. Matter, from its inferior nature,
cannot destroy it. Nor can any more powerful spiritual
being ; for one mind is subject to another only in so far
as its own will may allow such subjection, and it is evi-
dent that no mind will desire its own destruction. Thus
the soul can be destroyed by nothing but the will of God.

If it be thought that the soul may die in the sense that,
though not destroyed, it may exist without life, Augustine
shows that such an idea involves contradiction in terms.
The soul is life, and the source of life to everything that
lives. "The mind, therefore, cannot die. For if it can be

without life, it is not mind, but something made alive by mind" (*non animus, sed animatum aliquid est*—De Imort. Animæ, cap. 9).

The argument from the natural "longing after immortality" is frequently insisted on by Augustine. All men, he says, desire to be happy, and happiness cannot be genuine unless its possessor also desires its continuance. Now no man can be truly happy unless he have what he desires; and so, life must be eternal or happiness cannot be attained. Thus nature demands immortality. If it be objected that this argument implies that all, including even the bad, must attain to happiness, Augustine answers that happiness is granted to the good, not because they desire to live happily, but because they desire to live well. Happiness is the reward of goodness; and since all do not desire a good life, all cannot obtain its reward.

CLAUDIAN MAMERTUS, about the year 470, wrote a treatise *De Statu Animæ*, in reply to an anonymous work, afterwards known to have been written by Faustus, Bishop of Regium in Gaul. Faustus had maintained that God alone is incorporeal; all created things are matter, the soul being composed of air. Mamertus answers from the Augustinian stand-point. According to Mr. Lewes, he has exhausted all the capital arguments whereby Descartes was thought to have established the doctrine of immaterialism. Omitting his discussion of various points not immediately connected with our subject, and his extensive array of authorities from philosophers, from ecclesiastical writers, and from Scripture, we present in the following sketch an outline of his reasoning :—

Man was made in the image of God, and, according to the admission of Faustus himself, the Divine nature is incorporeal. Now since there can be no resemblance to God in matter, we must believe that this image is to be found in an immaterial soul. Moreover, the immaterial is of a higher nature than the material; and since the Deity is infinitely good, he will desire to create beings of the highest dignity, without which his works would be incomplete, and, being omnipotent, he will carry out this desire.

Again, the soul is not limited by place (*illocalis.*) It is wholly present in every part of the body as well as in the whole, just as God is present through the whole universe ; otherwise a portion of it would be lost when any part of the body is cut off. Whereas no material object can be present in more than one place at the same time, the soul at once animates the body, and as a whole sees through the eye, hears through the ear, &c. Its motion is not in space ; it takes place only in time ; being simply, as he explains, the change of thoughts and feelings. When the body moves, this local motion is not communicated to the soul.

The soul has no quantity, for place and quantity are inseparable. While no being except God is entirely beyond the sphere of the Categories (Aristotelian), it is only matter that is subject to them all ; thus the soul has quality but not quantity. In one sense, indeed, it has measure, number, and weight ; but then *measure* must be understood of degrees of wisdom ; *number* as the mental perception of external numbers; and *weight* must be applied to the will as the moving power in the mind.

The soul is not contained by the body, says Mamertus, but in reality contains it—as had already been taught by Plotinus. This point he endeavours to prove by Scripture, and then applies it to show that the soul must be immaterial ; for no material substance can at once contain the body, and be within it as its animating principle. If it be thought a contradiction that the soul is in a place and yet is not bounded by place, Mamertus replies that the universe itself presents a similar difficulty ; it cannot be contained in any place, else that place would require another, and so on till we should have to attribute to it the Divine perfection of infinity.

In addition to all these considerations, Mamertus also mentions the argument—previously employed by Augustine, and afterwards by Descartes—that Reasoning is inherent in the substance of the soul; and as reason is incorporeal, so also is the soul. In a similar manner he also argues from the will and the memory.

In refuting the arguments of Faustus, Mamertus displays force and ingenuity. Thus he fully examines the argument from the corporeal allusions in the parable of Lazarus and Dives. He shows that if these allusions prove the materiality of the soul, they must all be taken in the most literal sense, which cannot be done without producing inconsistencies and absurdities.

NEMESIUS, Bishop of Emesa, in Phœnicia (who flourished about the year 450), deserves mention as having had an influence in establishing Immaterialism in the Eastern Church.   He wrote a work on the nature of the Soul, in which he occupies chiefly the ground of Neo-Platonism. He holds that the soul is an immaterial substance.   It is involved, as Plato had taught, in eternal self-produced motion, from which the motion of the body is derived. He maintains the pre-existence of the soul, and holds that its nature, as supra-sensible, involves immortality.

From the fifth century down to the great development of Scholasticism, headed by Thomas Aquinas, in the thirteenth, there occurred no important changes of view in connexion with our subject.   In this latter period it again emerges into prominence, but now the point of view is changed.   All the reasonings of the Schoolmen were cast in the moulds of the Aristotelian philosophy, and cannot be understood until Aristotle's leading modes of thought and expression are first comprehended.   (See above under ARISTOTLE, especially the explanations of *Form* and *Matter*, *Actuality* and *Potentiality*.)   Thus, although Aquinas was a decided immaterialist, he does not aim, like Augustine and Claudian Mamertus, to show that the soul is without the material attributes of extension, quantity, &c.; he endeavours to prove that it is, in the Aristotelian sense, the Actuality of the body and pure immaterial Form. Hence in order to trace the development of the views culminating in Aquinas, we must recur to Aristotle.

The course from Aristotle to Aquinas is shown in the following summary from Ueberweg. "Aristotle regarded as Form (his highest abstraction and antithesis to matter), immaterial, and yet individual, the Deity, and the Active Nous or Intellect—the only immortal part of the human soul; leaving uncertain the relation between this immortal Nous and the mortal compound of soul and body. Among his immediate followers, as Dicæarchus and Strato, the prevailing view was that all Form is immanent in matter. Alexander the Aphrodisian ascribes to Deity, but to Deity only, a transcendental existence, free from matter, and yet individual; he makes the human soul depend entirely on matter for its individual existence. The later commentators, given over to Neo-Platonism, as Themistius, assert the human Nous to have the same independent and individual existence as the Deity. On this side Thomas Aquinas ranges himself."

ALBERTUS MAGNUS (1193—1280) deserves to be mentioned in this connection as having influenced the opinions of his pupil Aquinas. He held that the Active Intellect is a part of the soul, being in each man the principle that confers Form and individuality. In this principle are

also contained the forces called by Aristotle, Nutritive and
Sentient, and hence these latter powers are separable
from the body and immortal.   Every human soul is
immortal by virtue of its community with God.

THOMAS AQUINAS (1225—1274) represents the highest
stage in the development of the Scholastic philosophy.
His views on the nature of the Soul are to be found in '
several of his numerous philosophical and theological
works, but they are most conveniently gathered from the
First Part of his *Summa Theologiæ*, where the points
are fully and systematically set forth.   The following
abstract includes only such of his opinions on the soul as
concern our present purpose.

In maintaining that the Soul is not material, he says it
is the primary source of life in all living beings.   Now
while body may be a secondary source of living operations,
as the eye, for example, is the source of vision, body *as
such* is not living or a source of life.   It must have this
power as body of a particular kind (*per hoc quod est tale
corpus*), and the source whence anything receives its
character is its Actuality.   "The soul, therefore, which is
the primary source of life, is not body, but the Actuality
of body; as heat, which is the source whence bodies are
made hot, is not body, but a sort of actuality of body."
(*Sum. Theol.* I. 75, 1.)

The soul of man is an independent substance.   For by
the intellect man cognizes the natures of *all* kinds of

bodies. This could not be, if the intellect were matter, since the thing knowing must have nothing in it of the nature of the objects known ; nor, if it cognizes by means of body, because the determinate nature of the medium would hinder it from knowing *all* kinds of bodies, just as a diseased eye distorts vision, or the colour of a vessel affects the colour of a liquid contained in it. Therefore the intellectual principle works by itself without connexion with the body ; and as only a substance can thus work by itself, the soul of man is an independent substance. But this does not apply to the souls of brutes ; for the sentient soul cannot work of itself, but requires the co-operation of the body.

Thomas holds, as already stated, that the soul is pure Form, entirely without matter. As regards the intellect in particular, it could not otherwise cognize the essence of things. Matter is the principle of individuality, and would prevent the intellect from cognizing the universal, just as the sentient powers, which operate through bodily organs, perceive only individual things.

While repudiating the Platonic doctrine of pre-existence, Aquinas maintained the immortality of the soul as flowing from its immateriality. It cannot perish by anything external to itself; for since it is fitting that the beginning and the end of existence should take place in similar ways, what has independent being, can perish only of itself. Nor can it perish in this way ; for because Form is Actuality (see above in ARISTOTLE), existence belong

N

to it from its very nature. "Matter perishes through being separated from its Form; but it is impossible that Form should be separated from itself; wherefore it is impossible that existing Form should cease to have being." (This is similar to the reasoning of Augustine given above, and the latter half of the argument is equivalent to the Platonic view in the *Phaedo* that life is inseparable from the very notion of the soul.) Besides, says Aquinas, adapting to his own modes of thought the argument from the longing of the soul after immortality, "everything naturally desires existence after its own manner, and in things having the faculty of knowing, desire follows knowledge. Now while sense can know existence only under the limits of space and time (*cognoscit esse sub hic et nunc*), the intellect apprehends it absolutely and with reference to all time. Hence beings having intellect naturally desire to exist always, and a natural desire cannot exist in vain." (*Sum. Theol.* I. 75, 6.)

So much for the essential nature of the soul. In a separate discussion, he considers the union of Soul and Body. Here he inquires whether the intellectual principle is united to the body as its Form. He reasons that whatever brings a thing into actuality is its Form; and the principle that makes the body living is the soul, from which it receives growth, feeling, motion, and also *understanding*. And unless the intellect thus stands to the body in the intimate relation of Form to matter, we cannot comprehend how its actions can be attributed to the man *as his*. The Platonic doctrine, that the soul stands to the body merely in the relation of its moving principle, is repudiated. Thomas adds to all this that the higher any Form is, the less is it mingled with matter, and the more does it excel matter in its operations. And as the human soul is the noblest of all' Forms, some part of its operations has no relation to matter, namely, the operations of the Intellect.

Following his master Albertus, Aquinas holds that the nutritive, the sentient, and the intellectual faculties are exercised by one and the same soul. He argues that otherwise a man would not be really one, for the unity of any object comes from the same Form that gives it being. Besides, their identity appears from the fact that any operation of the soul, when intensely carried on, hinders any other. Thus the higher Form really includes the lower one—the sentient and the nutritive souls of Aristotle. (This opinion received dogmatic sanction at the Council of Vienne, in 1311).

Aquinas holds the idea, originated by Plotinus, that the whole soul is present in the whole and in every part of the body. But he characteristically distinguishes *three kinds* of totality. The soul is not present in each part as a whole in any quantitative sense, nor is it present in the wholeof its powers. This presence as a whole in each part must be understood as a presence of its whole nature and essence.

In discussing the faculties of the soul, Thomas argues that they do not all remain when the soul is separated from the body. Some powers are connected with the soul alone, as intellect and will; and these remain in the incorporeal state. Others are joined to the body, as the sentient and nutritive parts; and these disappear as to actual operation, when their bodily organs perish, though they still potentially remain in the soul. The Intellect is divided, after Aristotle, into Active, Theorizing, or Reproductive (*intellectus agens*); and Passive, or Receptive (*intellectus patiens*). An Active Intellect is necessary in order that the Forms of material things, which are mingled with matter, may be made intelligible in Actuality. This Active Intellect belongs to the soul; for though we may suppose (according to the Platonic view) a higher and separate Intellect, in which the Intellect of man participates—which Aquinas in one sense admits, making the Deity such an Intellect—yet we must suppose that this participation gives the human Intellect the power of separating the universal from the particular; which is to concede the operation of an Active Intellect within the soul.

The following diagram exhibits the transition from Aristotle to Aquinas. Let the continuous lines represent the material substance, and the dotted lines the immaterial. Aristotle's scheme stands thus :—

A. *Soul of Plants.*
——————— Without Consciousness.

B. *Animal Soul.*
– – – . – – – Body and Mind inseparable.

C. *Human Soul—NOUS—Intellect.*
I. Passive Intellect.
. . . . Body and Mind inseparable.

II. Active Intellect—Cognition of the highest principles ;
. . . . Pure Form ; detached from matter ; the Celestial substance ; immortal.

Compare the position of Aquinas :—

A. *Vegetable or Nutritive Soul.*
. . . . Incorporates an Immaterial part, although unconscious.

B. *Animal Soul.*
– – . . . . Has an Immaterial part, with consciousness.

C. *Intellect.*
. . . . Purely Immaterial.

DUNS SCOTUS (in the end of the thirteenth century) drew back somewhat from the extreme position of Aquinas. He held that God alone is absolutely pure Form ; all created beings, including angels and the soul, are composed of form and matter. The matter of the soul, however, is very different from the matter that constitutes bodies ; it is a created something, the basis of all finite existence, including corporeal matter itself.

But this protest was without effect. Aquinas had

triumphed ; the utmost limit of abstraction in the line of dualism had been reached.

Coming down now to modern times, we have to recognize Descartes as, by pre-eminence, the philosopher of Immaterialism (the word Spirituality is not used by him). Still, it is not unlikely that John Calvin, who preceded him by a century, had a considerable share in making this the creed of religious orthodoxy.

CALVIN substantially adopted the settlement of Aquinas. His views are found in his "Institutes," and in a short treatise " On the Sleep of the Soul," written against the doctrine that the soul is unconscious between death and the resurrection, a view that some of the Reformers were inclined to, in their opposition to purgatory. We follow Calvin's phraseology in the "Institutes." The Soul is an immortal essence, the nobler part of man ; it is a creation out of nothing, not an emanation ; it is essence without motion, not motion without essence. Its power of distinguishing good and evil, the swiftness and wide range of its faculties (so opposed to the brutes), the power of conceiving the invisible God,—are evidences that it is incorporeal, being incompatible with body. Then as to the vexed connexion with space : the soul is not properly bounded by space ; still it occupies the body as a habitation, animating its parts and endowing its organs for their several functions. The strength of Calvin's reasoning is still the " point-of-honour " argument.

Now for DESCARTES. It is not uncommon to style him the father of modern mental philosophy, so forcibly did he insist on the fundamental and inerazible distinction between matter and mind. Matter, whose essence is Extension, is known by the senses, and is so studied by the physical observer; mind, whose essence is Thinking, can be known only by self-consciousness, the organ or faculty of the metaphysical observer. He made the distinction (which Reid dwelt so much upon in his "Inquiry") between the mental element and the physical element in sensation; the feeling that we call heat being one thing, the physical property of the fire being a different thing. He stated it as a cardinal principle that nothing conceivable by the power of the imagination could throw any light on the operations of thought; which was merely stating, that the feelings and thoughts of the mind were something very different from a tree, a field, a river, or a palace, or anything else in the extended world. He argues for the Immateriality of the mental aggregate, or thinking principle.

Descartes was not without his theory of the physical accompaniments of the immaterial principle. He assigned to the soul a definite centre or locality in the brain, namely, the small body near the base called the pineal gland. He explained the mode of action of the brain by the flow of animal spirits along the nerves; but then the effect of these animal spirits was confined to the manifestations of our animal life, and did not connect themselves with the thinking principle or the proper soul. It is well known that he refused mind to animals, treating them as automatous or machines. In the fifth chapter of his "Discourse on Method," he goes very fully into what he considers the impassable distinctions between man and the brutes.

For his clear conception of the difference between matter and mind, Descartes deserves all praise ; that was to establish a fact. His appended doctrine of an immaterial substance is an hypothesis, for which, even if argument would suffice to make it intelligible and tenable, his arguments were singularly inadequate. He gives the often-repeated distinction between the divisibility of matter and the indivisibility of mind ; but although this could impose even upon Bishop Butler, it was blown to tatters like a cobweb by the materialists. True, a lump of brass is divisible ; but make it into a watch, and you can no longer split it into two without destroying it as a watch. You can no more cut a man's brain into two working brains than you can bisect his intelligence.

The great rival of Descartes in his own time was HOBBES, with whom substance was body, or matter, and nothing else. Spirit meant only a subtle invisible fluid, or æther (whose existence, however, he took no account of in his philosophy) ; or else it was a ghost, or mere phantom of imagination. But we must go on to the eighteenth century aspect of the question.

LOCKE'S allusions to the subject are characterized by his usual sagacity and sobriety. He cannot see that we are in any way committed to the immaterial nature of mind, inasmuch as Omnipotence might, for anything we know, as easily annex the power of thinking to matter directly, as to an immaterial substance to be itself annexed to matter. These are his words:—"He who will give himself leave to consider freely, and look into the dark and intricate part of each hypothesis, will scarcely find his reason able to determine him fixedly for or against the soul's materiality."

About the close of Locke's career, begins the great materialistic campaign of the last century, which may be said to culminate in Priestley. Before Priestley, the most important names on his side (the materialist) were Toland and Collins; while Samuel Clarke, a leader of the opposition, attacked more especially the materialism of the now forgotten Dodwell. Priestley had to contend with Price, whom he always treated with respect, and with Baxter, an extreme spiritualist, now a shade. Bishop Butler had argued for spiritualism in his "Analogy," but had contributed nothing new to the defence. It will be enough for us to advert to the Priestley stage of the English controversy; but first let us dispose of De la Mettrie and the continental materialists, who belong to the earlier half of the century.

DE LA METTRIE is introduced to us by Carlyle, among

the boon companions of Frederick, in the early part of his reign. He was a *bon vivant*, a diner-out, and a wit, as well as a philosopher; and his tragical end has no doubt been often used as a moral against too great fondness for good eating. His books, "Man a Machine," "Man a Plant," are written with much vivacity and cleverness of illustration, and were well suited to make an impression upon the more sceptical of his contemporaries. They are mainly made up of copious illustrations of the influence exercised over the feelings by physical conditions, such, for example, as food, stimulants, &c. " What a vast power there is in a repast ! Joy revives in a disconsolate heart; it is transfused into the souls of all the guests, who express it by amiable conversation or music." Again : " Raw meat gives fierceness to animals, and would do the same to man. This is so true that the English, who eat their meat underdone, seem to partake of this fierceness more or less, as shown in pride, hatred, contempt of other nations." So, " Man has been broken and trained by degrees, like other animals. . . . We are what we are by our organization in the first instance, and by instruction in the second. . . . Man is framed of materials, not exceeding in value those of other animals ; nature has made use of one and the same paste—she has only diversified the ferment in working it up. . . . We may call the body an enlightened machine. . . . It is a clock, and the fresh chyle from the food is the spring.' He goes slightly into the question whether matter has an inherent activity, adducing examples in the affirmative; but we shall see this position better argued by Priestley. He will not undertake to decide the existence of a Deity, the arguments for and against are so nearly balanced in his mind, and he is equally uncertain about Immortality; but he thinks materialism the most intelligible doctrine, as contenting itself with one substance, the most comfortable to entertain, and *the most calculated to promote universal benevolence.*

A similar strain of argument, with less wit and more logical concatenation, appears in the "Système de la Nature" of Baron d'HOLBACH; but we need not occupy space with him.

JOSEPH PRIESTLEY, besides being a voluminous and able writer on theology, mental philosophy, history, and many other things, was a distinguished experimenter in physical science, as his well-known discoveries attest. He commences his work on "Materialism" by an appeal to what was emphatically the eighteenth-century logic—not the logic of Aristotle, nor even of Bacon, but the logic of Newton: for Newton was a logician by precept no less than by example; his four rules of philosophizing were not merely given at the outset of every work on natural philosophy, but were laid to heart and acted out by scientific inquirers. Priestley was also, in consequence of his scientific studies, the fit man to deal with the crude and inaccurate notion, adduced as an argument for spiritualism

(8), that matter is a solid, impenetrable, inert substance, and wholly passive and indifferent to rest or motion, except as acted on by some power foreign to itself. In opposition to this view, he shows that matter is essentially gifted with active properties, with powers of attraction and repulsion; even its impenetrability involves repulsive forces. Indeed, he is disposed to adopt the theory of Boscovich, which makes matter nothing else than an aggregate of centres of force, of points of attraction and repulsion, one towards the other. The inherent activity of matter being thus vindicated, why should it not be able to sustain the special activity of thought, seeing that sensation and perception have never been found but in an organized system of matter? It being a rigid canon of the Newtonian logic, not to multiply causes without necessity, we should adhere to a single substance until it be shown, which at present it cannot, that the properties of mind are incompatible with the properties of matter. In following out his argument, he presents a well-digested summary of the facts referring to the concomitance of body and mind; and cleverly retorts the doctrine that the body impedes the exercise of our powers, by remarking that, on that theory, our mental powers should be steadily increasing as we approach to dissolution. He urges the difficulties of having an immaterial and unextended substance joined with matter in the relation of place, as well as mechanically acting upon matter—points that had never indeed been cleared up to the satisfaction of the immaterialists

themselves. As the Fathers had often said, there can be no
mutual influence where there is no common property. He
is especially indignant at the practice of shielding absurdity
under the venerable name of "mystery." He would doubt-
less have applied Newton's rule against multiplying causes,
to forbid the multiplying of mysteries without necessity.
And, in general, as to a spiritual substance, the vulgar, like
the ancients and the first Fathers, will never be able to
see the difference between it and nothing at all. He then
takes up the Scripture view of the question, endeavouring
to prove that the language of the Old Testament implies
only a single substance with spiritual properties or
adjuncts; that the same view is most conformable to the
New Testament; and that the doctrine of a separate soul
embarrasses the whole system of Christianity. Of course he
will not admit a middle state, between death and the
resurrection; nor that such a state apart from the body
has anything to do with the immortality of the soul, which
doctrine he rests exclusively on the Scripture testimony
to a general resurrection.

Such is a summary of by far the ablest defence of the
single-substance doctrine in the last century. It became
the creed of great numbers at the end of that century and
the beginning of this. The celebrated Robert Hall was for
many years a materialist in Priestley's sense; and the occasion of his ceasing to be so can hardly be considered as a
refutation of the doctrine. He says of himself, that "he
buried his materialism in his father's grave."

Coming down to the present century, we may take DUGALD STEWART as a fair representative of the metaphysicians. We find him repudiating materialism; but when we inquire what he understands by it, we see that he really means the confounding of mind and matter under one common phenomenon, or one set of properties—the material properties; as in an unguarded phrase of Hume's, "that little agitation of the brain that we call thought;" for though an agitation of the brain *accompanies* thought, it is not itself the thought.* Stewart says that "although we have the strongest evidence that there is a thinking and sentient principle within us essentially distinct from matter, yet we have no direct evidence of the possibility of this principle exercising its various powers in a separate state from the body. On the contrary, the union of the two, while it subsists, is evidently of the most intimate nature." And he goes on to adduce some of the strong facts that show the dependence of mind on body.

---

* It is not often that either single-substance materialism or double materialism is exemplified by moderns, except through incaution in the use of language. Robert Hooke (quoted by Dr. Reid, "Intellectual Powers," Essay II., chap ix.) indulges in a materialistic strain, not unlike some of the ancient philosophers. "In his lectures upon Light, he makes ideas to be material substances; and thinks that the brain is furnished with a proper kind of matter, for fabricating the ideas of each sense. The ideas of sight, he thinks, are formed of a kind of matter resembling the Bononian stone, or some kind of phosphorus."

A materialism of this kind pervades Darwin's *Zoonomia*, from which the following expressions are quoted by Mill ("Logic," Fallacies, chap. iii. § 8) :—The word *idea* " is defined a contraction, a motion, or configuration, of the fibres which constitute the immediate organ of sense;" "our *ideas* are animal motions of the organ of sense."

He says that the mental philosopher is rightly occupied in ascertaining " the laws that regulate their connexion, without attempting to explain in what manner they are united."

The late Professor FERRIER, who in his "Institutes of Metaphysics" has set forth, in a nomenclature of his own, the contrast or antithesis of mind and matter, bestows a somewhat contemptuous handling on the common-place spiritualism. We quote his words :—

" In vain does the spiritualist found an argument for the existence of a separate immaterial substance on the alleged incompatibility of the intellectual and the physical phenomena to co-inhere in the same sub-stratum. Materiality may very well stand the brunt of that unshotted broadside. This mild artifice can scarcely expect to be treated as a serious observation. Such an hypothesis cannot be meant to be in earnest. Who is to dictate to nature what phenenoma, or what qualities inhere in what substances; what effects may result from what causes? Matter is already in the field as an acknowledged entity—this both parties admit. Mind, considered as an independent entity, is not so unmistakably in the field ! Therefore, as entities are not to be multiplied without necessity, we are not entitled to postulate a new cause, so long as it is *possible* to account for the phenomena by a cause already in existence ; which possibility has never yet been disproved."

HAMILTON remarks that we cannot localize the mind, without clothing it with the attributes of extension and place ; and to make the seat or locality a point only aggravates the difficulty. We have no right to limit it to any part of the organism; the mind cannot be denied to feel at the finger points. The sum of our knowledge of the connexion of mind and body is—that the mental modifications are dependent on certain corporeal conditions ; but of the nature of these conditions we know nothing. (Lectures on Metaphysics, ii., 127.)

The reply may be given to Hamilton that, in one signification of the words, it is correct to say that we know nothing of the corporeal conditions of mind, namely, that they are generically distinct from mind itself ; that they cannot be resolved into mind, and mind cannot be resolved into them. In another signification, however, we know a great deal respecting these material conditions, and may one day know all that is to be known about them. Indeed, something has been known from the very beginning of human observation.

It is quite true, as Hamilton remarks, that to localize mind is to run into contradiction and absurdity. This, however, may be averted by adapting our phraseology to the peculiar nature of the things ; in speaking of mind, we must avoid the language of extension or place.

MANSEL (Prolegomena Logica, p. 198) remarks :—" To this day we are ignorant how matter and mind operate on each other. We know not how the material refractions of the eye are connected with the mental sensation of seeing, nor how the determination of the will operates in bringing about the motion of the muscles." Here there is the erroneous assumption that power or efficiency belongs to mind in the abstract. Assume the alliance of mind and matter, and there is nothing hopeless in seeking an explanation of their mutual action. The alliance itself is an unaccountable, because an ultimate, fact ; of it no explanation is competent or relevant, except generalizing it to the uttermost.

Again, says Mansel, "We can investigate severally the phenomena of matter and mind, as we can severally the constitution of the earth, and the architecture of the heavens ; we seek the boundary line of their junction, as the child chases the horizon, only to discover that it flies as we pursue it." The mistake is in looking for a boundary line at all. We look for a boundary between two parishes, two estates, two adjoining tissues of the animal framework ; but between the extended body, and the unextended mind, the search for a boundary line is incompetent and unmeaning.

I now pass to the latest phase of this eventful history.

A movement in favour of Materialism has arisen in Germany within the last twenty years ; which is in part a re-action from the high-flown philosophy that so long prevailed, and in part an application to mind of the physical science of this century, as Priestley in his day applied the physical science of the last century.

It is to be remarked, however, that spiritualism, in the form of dualism, was never the philosophic creed of Germany. Kant, who ridiculed alike materialism and idealism, yet did not ascribe to matter a real existence by the side of an independent spiritual principle. Fichte and Hegel, being over-mastered with the idea of unity, had to make a choice; and attaching themselves by preference to the dignified mental side, became pantheists of an ideal school; resolving all existence into mind or ideas. People generally, when tired of Kant's critical position, became either materialists, or idealists, and not believers in two substances.

As regards the recent materialistic movement, scientific men first broke ground. Emphatic utterances were made by such men as Müller, Wagner, Liebig, and Du Bois Reymond, all tending to rehabilitate the powers of matter. But the outspoken and thorough-going materialism begins with Moleschott, who in 1852, published his "Circular Course of Life," a series of letters addressed to Liebig. In 1854, Vogt came into the field, in an attack upon Wagner, the great physiologist, who had said that, although nothing in physiology suggested a distinct soul, yet this tenet was demanded by man's moral relations. In a series of subsequent works, Vogt has urged the dependence of mind on body in extreme and unnecessarily offensive language. The third and most popular expounder of these views is Büchner, in his book "Matter and Force," which was first published in 1856, has run through a great many editions, and has been also translated into English.

It is not necessary to expatiate upon the views of these writers. Their handling turns partly on the accumulated proofs, physiological and other, of the dependence of mind on body, and partly upon the more recent doctrines as to matter and force, summed up in the grand generality known as the Correlation, Conservation, or Persistence of Force. This principle enables them to surpass Priestley in the cogency of their arguments for the essential and inherent activity of matter; all known force being in fact embodied in matter. Their favourite text is "no matter without force, and no force without matter." The notion of a quiescent impassive block, called matter, coming under the influence of forces *ab extra*, or superimposed, is, they hold, less tenable now than ever. Are not the motions of the planets maintained by the inherent power of matter? And, besides the two great properties called Inertia and Gravity, every portion of matter has a certain temperature, consisting, it is believed, of intestine motions of the atoms, and able to exert force upon any adjoining matter that happens to be of a lower temperature. Then they ask with Priestley and Ferrier: "Why introduce a new entity, or rather a nonentity, until we see what these multifarious activities of matter are able to accomplish?" They also reply to the spiritualistic argument based on the personal identity of the mind and the constant flux of the body, by the obvious remark, that the body has its identity too, in *type* or form, although the constituent molecules may change and be replaced.

It is not to be supposed that these writers are in the ascendant in Germany, or that their language is always metaphysically guarded. Still, having written intelligible books, easily appealing to a palpable and determinate class of facts, they have been extensively read; and their ideas or the scientific facts that they are based on, are modifying even the highest transcendentalism of that remarkable country.

The rapid sketch thus given seems to tell its own tale as to the future. The arguments for the two substances have, we believe, now entirely lost their validity; they are no longer compatible with ascertained science and clear thinking. The one substance, with two sets of properties, two sides, the physical and the mental—a *double-faced unity*—would appear to comply with all the exigencies of the case. We are to deal with this, as in the language of the Athanasian Creed, not confounding the persons nor dividing the substance. The mind is destined to be a double study—to conjoin the mental philosopher with the physical philosopher; and the momentary glimpse of Aristotle is at last converted into a clear and steady vision.

BRADBURY, AGNEW & CO., WHITEFRIARS.